A Legendary Force

1st Patiala

300 Years of 15 Punjab (Patiala)

THE FOUNDER

BABA ALA SINGH

THE FOUNDER
OF PATIALA STATE
(1705-1765)

A Legendary Force
1st Patiala

300 Years of 15 Punjab (Patiala)

Colonel Anil Shorey

Manas Publications
New Delhi - 110 002 (India)

MANAS PUBLICATIONS
(Publishers, Distributors, Importers & Exporters)
4858, Prahlad Street,
24, Ansari Road, Darya Ganj,
New Delhi - 110 002 (INDIA)
Ph.: 23260783, 23265523 (O); 27131660(R)
Fax: 011- 23272766
E-mail: manaspublications@vsnl.com

© Colonel Anil Shorey (Retd.)
2005

ISBN 81-7049-246-7
Rs. 495/-

No part of this book can be reproduced, stored in a retrieval system, or transmitted in any form, by any means, including mechanical, electronic, photocopying, recording, or otherwise, without prior written permission of the publisher.

The views expressed in this book are those of the author and not necessarily of the publisher. The publisher is not responsible for the views of the author and authenticity of the data, in any way what so ever.

Typeset at
Manas Publications

Printed in India at
Nice Printing Press
and Published by Mrs. Suman Lata for
Manas Publications, 4858, Prahlad Street
24, Ansari Road, Daryaganj
New Delhi 110002 (INDIA)

To late Brigadier Sukhdev Singh, VrC, MC, former commanding officer and hero of Zojila; to Major SPS Waraich who went missing during the 1971 Hussainiwala battle, presumed to have been taken captive by Pakistani forces; to my respected father, late Lieutenant Colonel I.K. Shorey who was commissioned into 15 Punjab but died in harness in NEFA while commanding 14 Punjab (Nabha Akal) in February 1963, and to all officers, JCOs and men of the gallant battalion who made the supreme sacrifice while upholding the honour of their unit, formation and the nation. To all of them, with respect and humility, I dedicate this book.

Foreword

I am happy to write the Foreword of this book, which narrates the history of 300 years of the famous battalion of the Indian army - 1st Patiala (Rajindra Sikhs), now known as 15 Punjab (Patiala). There is no denying that the chequered history of this legendary battalion has no parallel; as a matter of fact it could be compared amongst the most decorated and reputed battalions in the world. It has undoubtedly carved out a niche for itself in most of the wars. It fought with élan during World War I at Suez, Port Said, Gaza, Amman, the Dardanelles and Palestine; after which it fought with distinction in the Third Afghan War. During World War II the Patialas fought in the North West Frontier Province (NWFP) and also took on the Japanese in the Burmese theatre. The Patialas not only turned the flanks of the Japanese columns operating east of the Chindwin, but also successfully neutralize many Japanese officer and men. After the armistice they moved to the Dutch East Indies, what is now known as Indonesia where they went on to prove their mettle.

Following India's partition the battalion was rushed to Jammu & Kashmir from Patiala where they took on the Pakistani marauders at Chhamb, Naushera and Jhangar. Their finest battle was fought at a the frozen heights of Zojila where they not only took on the Pakistani battalion known as Gilgit Scouts but also succeeded in pushing them beyond Dras and Kargil thus facilitating a link up of Indian troops advancing from the valley with the besieged garrison of Leh. The unit earned eight Maha Vir Chakras and eighteen Vir Chakras during this war, an unmatched record established by any battalion during any war till date.

This legendary battalion fought heroically at Hussainiwala in the Fazilka Sector during the 1971 war. Fighting against a brigade of enemy infantry supported by armour, the battalion put on a determined stance in spite of extremely heavy odds, and, in the process it suffered considerable casualties but not without unnerving and subsequently halting the enemy thrust on the western banks of River Sutlej. Thereafter the unit continued to excel in various other fronts, be it fighting the vagaries of the weather; the inhospitable and rugged terrain of high altitude areas or combating terrorists.

The saga of Dalunanag near Dras in the high altitude area of Ladakh in Jammu & Kashmir speaks volumes of the heroic exploits of the battalion where they succeeded in evicting Pakistani intruders from dominating heights along the Line of Control during 1988-89. Three years later the Patialas again established a record of sorts when they took on the terrorist's head on in the most volatile and densely infested areas of Baramula and Sopore in the Kashmir valley. Here not only did the battalion subdue the terrorists but also earned a number of honours and awards to include one Kirti Chakra, two Shaurya Chakras and 47 other awards, apart from earning the coveted COAS's Unit Citation and GOC-in-C's Unit Appreciation. The achievements in other fields such as sports and professional competitions also speak volumes of the battalion's overall composition and framework. Today the 1st Patialas have more than 330 assorted honours and awards to its credit and the unit remains in peak form to take on other challenges in various

Foreword

fronts with élan and missionary zeal, as it has done during the past 300 years.

Colonel Anil Shorey (Retd), a second generation officer of the Punjab Regiment and a former commanding officer of 15 Punjab (Patiala), has carried out detailed research of the rich history of this unique battalion. He has painstakingly compiled all avaliable material and woven it into a most pleasantly readable and well compiled book form. With a rich content of rare photographs and crisp maps, the appeal of the book has been further enhanced thereby making its reading alongwith comprehension a most pleasant experience. I hope the book will be read by all members of not only the 1st Patiala fraternity but also by all those of the Punjab Regiment and the entire Indian army per se, to include all serving and retired personnel alongwith members of their families, particularly the youth. On the occasion of the tercentenary of 15 Punjab (Patiala), I wish all those associated with the battalion at any time the best of luck, good wishes and a great future ahead. God bless.

Wahe Guru Ji Ka Khalsa, Sri Wahe Guru Ji Ki Fateh.

**Lieutenant General Mohinder Singh,
PVSM, UYSM, AVSM
Adjutant General and
Colonel of the Punjab Regiment**

Preface

I consider myself truly fortunate to have been given the singular honour by my Regiment and battalion to write this book. The last three centuries have seen my battalion earning a galaxy of laurels and attaining invaluable heights. In fact 15 Punjab (Patiala) stands tall and towering amongst its various co-battalions of the Indian army. Over the years it has established a record of sorts and earned a legendary reputation through its untiring and unstinted efforts during war and peace. The atmosphere within the battalion has always remained charged, electrifying and vibrant in a positive way, radiating a similar aura around it as well. Forever 'go getters' and most positive in their attitude, the Patialas have never said 'no' to accept any challenge or to lend out a helping hand to needy colleagues or units. So much needs to be said of this legendary battalion that I find it difficult to restrain myself from doing so in this preface. I consider it best to leave the discovering of the battalion to the readers of this book who, I am sanguine, will not be disappointed.

It has been my honest endeavour to project the various facets, activities and achievements of this veteran battalion in as simple and readable a manner as possible.

The history of the battalion has been painfully yet enthusiastically compiled through various sources, and chronicled theatre and subject-wise. A suitable background has also been given such as the prevailing situation existing before narrating a battle or operation. All this has been done to facilitate the readers to perceive the larger picture of the vast battalion mosaic at any given time.

I am also grateful to many regimental peers and various commanding officers for rendering me invaluable advice and specific information from time to time, without which it would have been well nigh impossible to complete this project in record time to coincide with the battalion's tricentenary. Although I was keen to complete the project while I was in command, the challenges of command and my frequent, high pressure postings thereafter prevented me from going beyond the keel of this book till after having shed my 'Galley' uniform on superannuating recently.

An earnest endeavour has also been made to ensure factual accuracies. However, all relevant data has been based on the plethora of inputs available with the battalion and volumes of letters and hand-written narratives handed over to me by many of our legendary peers and seniors, most of whom I have thanked and acknowledged in this book.

Bon voyage and happy reading.

Col Anil Shorey (Retd.)

Acknowledgement

I am grateful to Lieutenant General Mohinder Singh, PVSM, UYSM, AVSM, the Colonel of the Punjab Regiment and to the Punjab Fraternity for giving me the opportunity and placing their trust in me for bringing out the 15 Punjab (Patiala) history book. It has been my earnest endeavour to come up to their expectations in every way.

I would also like to express my gratitude to some of the veteran officers / commanding officers of 15 Punjab (Patiala), particularly to late Brigadier Sukhdev Singh, VrC, MC; Major General Shivdev Singh (now retired), Colonels Shamsher Singh, Rajinder Singh Grewal, PS Vasudevan and Inderjit Singh, Lieutenant Colonel RP Singh, Captain Ramesh Chander Chhokra (all retired) and to all my colleagues and well wishers of the 1st Patiala fraternity, the list of which is endless. I would also like to express my deepest gratitude to Col S P Singh (AOC), brother of late Maj S P S Waraich of the Battalion (who remains missing since the 1971 war) for making available a copy of the book 'Patiala & the Great War', Medici Society, London, 1923, which proved to be of immense help.

The late Brigadier Sukhdev Singh, to whom I have dedicated this book, has truly been the driving force behind this project. Not only has he provided tremendous encouragement and a plethora of material to me through numerous publications, articles, and painstakingly hand written letters, but also his warmth, sincerity of purpose, a vast reservoir of knowledge and paternal love shown towards me have left an indelible impression in my mind and an irreparable scar deep within me following his demise. In his loss I found a painful void, akin to when I lost my own father when I was just a little over 12 years of age. Men and soldiers like him are rare to find today. He was an officer and a gentleman at the same time, apart from being an outstanding commanding officer and the true guiding spirit of the battalion. Of course, he was also the hero of Zojila. No words of praise for this legendary man are enough, and I, alongwith my 1st Patiala colleagues, pray for eternal peace to his departed soul.

I would also like to thank Havildar Clerk N.M. Samota of 15 Punjab (Patiala) and Sepoy Clerk Inderjit Singh of the Rajput Regiment, without whose invaluable assistance this venture may not have seen the light of day.

Wahe Guru Ji Ka Khalsa,· Sri Wahe Guru Ji Ki Fateh.

Col. Anil Shorey(Retd.)

Contents

Foreword   7
Preface   11
Acknowledgement   13

1. Origin of Modern Indian Army   17
2. The Inception of 1st Patiala   27
3. The Maturing   30
4. New Shape and Conquests   33
5. 1st Patiala During World War I   42
6. Between the Wars   70
7. The Patialas in World War II   73
8. Operations in Jammu & Kashmir (1947-48)   96
9. After the War   152
10. Indo-Pak War—1971   156
11. The Post-1971 War Era   169

12.	Battle of Dalunang	172
13.	Towards Countering the Proxy War	178
14.	In the Western Sector	202
15.	Other Fronts	205
	Epilogue	216
	Index	*229*

1

Origin of Modern Indian Army

Before narrating the rich and chequered history of one of the finest and most decorated battalions of the Indian army, 15 Punjab (Patiala), it will be befitting to understand the inception, structure and restructuring of the modern-day Indian army, apart from that of the various State Force armies, the origin of which goes back much before the regular army.

The regular army undoubtedly owes its origin to the British East India Company and its three presidencies, viz., Madras, Bengal and Bombay. Before tracking their origin I am reminded of the words of the former President of India, Dr. Zakir Hussain who paid a glowing tribute to the famous Punjab Regiment during its colour presentation at Meerut in March 1969. He said: "Your regiment has the single honour of being the oldest infantry regiment of the Indian army, and therefore the history of the Punjab Regiment is the history of the Indian Army."

The Evolution of Indian Army

The history of the Punjab Regiment has its genesis in the very evolution of the regular army in India. In any case, the ancient record of any regiment can hardly be written without, at least, a cursory glance into the history of the very army to which it belongs. The first authentic record of the existence of a sort of regular battalion on Indian soil dates back to the year 1741, when such a unit came into being for carrying out garrison duties in Bombay Castle. Seven years later Major Stringer Lawrence, 'the father of the Indian Army', was appointed Commander-in-Chief of the East India Company's field forces in India with its headquarters at Fort St. David, 100 miles south of Madras township and only 12 miles from the then French town of Pondicherry. The war with France, which had temporarily ended in 1748, had brought about a substancial increase in the local enrolment of Indian troops, since neither France nor Britain could spare regular troops for India. In 1754, however, a considerable force of King's troops was sent to India from England, but this again proved to be woefully inadequate to manage the Company's military affairs in India, and local recruitment continued.

In 1757, the reorganisation of the Indian troops into regular, organised battalions was entrusted by Major Lawrence to Robert Clive. That year is also famous for the Battle of Plassey, which gradually reduced French influence and led to an expansion of the Company's territories in India. With the expansion, the number of troops at its disposal, quite naturally, increased. Thus came into being the first regular Indian infantry battalions, each with an establishment of one British captain, two lieutenants, several British sergeants, 42 Indian non-commissioned officers and 820 Indian ranks and file. Clive was the first British officer in India to have Indian troops fully equipped, at the expense of the East India Company, which was popularly known as 'Sarkar'. He even dressed them with British 'Red Coats', hence the term 'Lal Paltan' came into being, which was locally used for such units, albeit with awe and pride.

Origin of Modern Indian Army

An important feature of this new organisation was that, although British elements were introduced into the Indian battalions, the Indian officers previously serving with them were still retained, and each battalion had its own Indian commandant. While the executive command and internal discipline of a battalion were entrusted to the Indian commandant and his team of Indian officers, tactical control and supervision of training were the responsibility of the British Captain and his two Lieutenants. However, towards the early part of the 19th century, the establishment of British officers in an Indian Infantry battalion was increased from the original three to as many as 22, a little below the officer strength of a British infantry battalion. This change naturally brought about a corresponding reduction in the number of Indian officers in a battalion, as a result of which the overall command was given to a British officer.

The Genesis of Punjab Regiment

Similarly, the earliest battalions of the Punjab Regiment came from south India. These had a class composition of troops from the then Madras Presidency, the oldest of the three presidencies of East India Company. The other two were Bengal and Bombay Presidencies. Gradually, as the British in India further expanded their influence, their regular Indian army units carried out a series of redesignations, each conforming to the region from where they recruited soldiers in their respective presidencies. Therefore, all the first five battalions, which in 1922 were regrouped as the 2nd Punjab Regiment, were raised between 1761 and 1798. Noteworthy is the fact that the first four battalions were raised during the hostilities in the Carnatic between 1761 and 1776. While the first three were raised as battalions of the Coast Sepoys, the fourth was raised as a Carnatic Battalion. The fifth was raised in

1798 as a battalion of Madras Native Infantry. As a matter of historical interest, the 2nd, 3rd and 4th Battalions fought with distinction under Sir Eyre Coote and acquired the first Battle Honour—'Sholinghur'—later to be borne on the Colour of the Regiment. Until 1784, there had been separate 'Circar' battalions and 'Carnatic' battalions, with the former serving in the north of the Madras Presidency and the latter in the south. This distinction was soon abolished, and all became Madras Native Infantry battalions. Further reorganisation became necessary in a gradual manner as the armies of the three presidencies expanded their influence, in terms of real estate, towards central India. As a matter of interest, battalions raised between 1757 and 1761, that is even before the first battalion of the Indian 2nd Punjab Regiment, were designated in a similar manner, albeit they subsequently formed part of the 1st Punjab Regiment, which is now in Pakistan, due to their greater seniority.

In 1824 all the first five battalions of the Indian Punjab Regiment were redesignated as 7, 9, 12, 14 and 27 battalions of Madras Native Infantry respectively. These numbers were retained until 1903, although their designation changed to Madras Infantry towards the middle of the century. In November 1902, Lord Kitchener became Commander-in-Chief and immediately set to work on further reorganisation and redistribution of the army in India. Since the recruitment pattern shifted further northwards towards the end of the 19th century, it again became necessary for Indian battalions to be given new names in 1903, names like Punjabis, Dogras, Marathas, Rajputs, Sikhs, Jats, Garhwalis, Moplahs and so on, depending on their recruiting pattern. Therefore, in 1903, the first five battalions of the Punjab Regiment were further redesignated as 'Punjabi' battalions. By adding a numerical

Origin of Modern Indian Army

60 to their Madras Infantry designation, these battalions then became 67, 69, 72, 74, and 87 'Punjabis' respectively. Similar was the pattern of redesignations in other Presidencies.

Indian Army's 'Grand Reorganisation' of 1922

This arrangement remained till 1922 when, under General Lord Rawlington's 'Grand Reorganisation', a group of battalions from a certain ethnic region of India formed a 'Regiment' with its own distinct dress code, badge, training centre or depots, customs and traditions. Each regiment was given a number based on the seniority of its battalions since raising and, similarly, each battalion was given a sub-number. The regiments thus created, seniority-wise, were 1 Punjab, 2 Punjab, 3 Madras, 4 Grenediers, 5 Maratha Light Infantry, 6 Rajputana Rifles, 7 Rajput, 8 Punjab, 9 Jat, 10 Baluch, 11 Sikh, 12 Frontier Force Regiment, 13 Frontier Force Rifles, 14 Punjab, 15 Punjab, 16 Punjab, 17 Dogra, 18 Garhwal, 19 Hyderabad, Assam, Gurkhas and so on. For instance, 3/2 Punjab represented the third battalion of the 2nd seniormost regiment of the Indian Army – 2nd Punjab. Accordingly in 1922 the five 'Punjabi' battalions were grouped together to form the 2nd Punjab Regiment and renumbered as 1/2, 2/2, 3/2, 4/2 and 5/2 Punjab Regiment respectively. The entire Indian army underwent a total restructuring in a similar manner. Thus in 1922 the modern Indian Army came into being in terms of regiments and corps.

The State Force Army

Ironically, prior to the inception of the Indian Army based on the British model, most of the Princely Indian States had their own armies to include infantry, artillery and cavalry units amongst other logistic units or sub-units. While expanding their influence over India, the British augmented their own armies through local recruitment in order to effectively fight some of these state armies who dared to oppose their advances. Noteworthy is the fact that state armies like those of Travancore, Cochin, Mysore, Kolhapur, Hyderabad, Berar, Indore, Baroda, Gwalior, Bhopal, Saurashtra, Jaipur, Jodhpur, Faridkot, Patiala, Jind, Nabha, Kapurthala, Cooch Behar and also Kashmir, to name a few, were well-trained and very well organised.

However, the British permitted a large number of these states to maintain their armies even after subduing them. With the establishment of the British power in most of India, the Indian states reconsolidated their armies with the implementation of the Subsidiary Alliance by Lord Wellesley, under which the Indian States were required to maintain forces for the use of the Imperial power. In some cases, where the states were unable to ensure regular finances for their forces, funds were provided and large tracts of land were ceded for their training, accommodation and maintenance. With increasing demands on the State Force armies, particularly during the two World Wars and numerous other campaigns overseas, their organisation and training were brought on the same lines as the regular Indian army. Later, States Force armies were termed Imperial Service Troops. To ensure a uniform standard, the Commander-in-Chief exercised a general supervision and control of these forces. For this purpose a nucleus staff was provided at the Army Headquarters, under a Military Adviser-in-Chief. He, in turn, was assisted by a Assistant Military Adviser. Many of these State Force units and sub-units performed splendidly in a number of campaigns in India and overseas, particularly in North West Frontier Province (NWFP) and during the two World Wars.

Origin of Modern Indian Army

Most of the State Force armies, to include those states which ceded to India following the partition of India, were amalgamated into the regular army after Independence. Between 1950 to 1954 they were all allotted the various regular infantry regiments, depending on their class composition, and were redesignated accordingly. For instance, with regards to the Punjab Regiment, the famous and battle scarred units or State Forces belonging to the erstwhile Patiala and East Punjab State's Union (PEPSU), such as the Jind infantry battalion, the Nabha State infantry battalion (known as Nabha Akal Infantry) and the 1st and 2nd Battalions of Patiala State were amalgamated with the Punjab Regiment and by mid-1954 they were redesignated as 13 Punjab (Jind), 14 Punjab (Nabha Akal), 15 Punjab (Patiala) and 16 Punjab (Patiala) respectively. The numerous other State Force battalions which went to various other regiments were redesignated in a similar manner.

Class Composition of Punjab Regiment

To recapitulate, the troops of the 2nd Punjab Regiment consisted of Sikhs, Dogras and Punjabi Mussalmans. The Regiment had flourished and earned an envious reputation on the basis of camaraderie and trust amongst its soldiers. This unique combination of troops had proved its worth in various operations under the British rule. During Partition in 1947, based on religious composition, many Muslim majority battalions and regiments were separated from the Indian army and went to Pakistan to form part of their army. Likewise many Muslim soldiers of the 2nd Punjab Regiment also migrated to Pakistan. During Partition, when the communal riots were at a peak, a safe passage was organised by a number of escort parties, consisting of Indian Punjabi troops, which ensured a safe passage across the border of Punjabi Muslims of the Regiment, thereby earning tremendous goodwill. Ironically, many battalions of the Punjab Regiment of India and Pakistan have fought with each other on a number of occasions during the various Indo-Pak wars.

After Independence, the 9th battalion was raised in 1948 by combining a Sikh company each from 5/12 Frontier Force Regiment (FF), who were the former famous 'Guides', the 8/12 FF Regiment and 1/14 Punjab Regiment, and a Dogra company each from 6/13 FF Rifles and 1/14 Punjab Regiment.

However, after Independence it was seen that the composition of many battalions, including those of the Punjab Regiment, varied from battalion to battalion. During the years 1955-60 the battalions of practically all the regiments were reorganized with a view to conform to their respective class composition pattern. Similarly the battalions of the Punjab Regiment were also reorganized on the Sikh-Dogra pattern by transferring men to other battalions and regiments, apart from granting release to those who sought it. There were, however, two exceptions. While 14 Punjab (Nabha Akal) was organised (and still is) on a 75% : 25% Sikh-Dogra composition, 15 Punjab (Patiala) was allowed to retain its wholly Sikh composition, which is being retained till date.

Present Status of the Regiment

In 1950, two of the Punjab Regiment's oldest battalions, i.e., 1 and 2 Punjab, were detached and formed the nucleus for the creation of the Parachute Regiment and the Brigade of the Guards respectively. They were redesignated as 1 Para (Punjab) (now Special Forces) and 1 Guard (Punjab) respectively. 7 Punjab, which became mechanized (Mech), also formed part of the newly created Mechanized Infantry

Origin of Modern Indian Army

Regiment and was redesignated 8 Mech (Punjab) in 1982. With new designations having been given to the PEPSU State Force battalions forming part of the Punjab Regiment, i.e. 13 Punjab (Jind), 14 Punjab (Nabha Akal), 15 and 16 Punjab (Patiala) respectively, 17 to 28 Punjab Battalions, two TA (Punjab) battalions and four Rashtriya Rifles (RR) (Punjab) battalions have been added to the regiment since 1962.

Regimental Performance

The performance of the various battalions of the Punjab Regiment during post-independence wars and campaigns has been of an exceptionally high order. During the Kashmir Operations of 1948, 15 Punjab (then known as Ist Patiala) saved Jammu & Kashmir by halting and later routing the raiders. Their finest moments were at the frozen heights of Zojila. This battalion established a record by earning eight Mahavir Chakras and 18 Vir Chakras in this theatre, a record unbroken till date. In the same theatre, 1 Guards (2 Punjab) proved its mettle once again at Naushera while 1 Para (Punjab) clinched Hajipir. During the Hyderabad Police Action that year, three battalions of the Regiment participated and did the Regiment proud. They were 3 Punjab, 7 Punjab and 9 Punjab. In the 1962 war against China, 9 Punjab acquitted itself in a commendable manner in erstwhile NEFA.

In 1965, the battle for the Ichhogil Canal brought glory to 7 Punjab, 13 Punjab (Jind) and 16 Punjab (Patiala). 19 Punjab earned undying fame at Bedori and Hajipir in the Poonch sector, while 9 Punjab secured a vital highway against determined Pakistani attacks at Kalidhar. In October that year, 3 Punjab did an year's stint overseas in Gaza, where it gave a sterling performance during the conduct of United Nations Peace Keeping Operations under the banner of United Nations Emergency Force (UNEF) between October '65 and October '66.

In the 1971 war, 14 Punjab (Nabha Akal) played a key role in the drive to Jessore and Khulna in Bangladesh, where it fought the famous Garibpur battle in which it destroyed 14 Pakistani Chaffee tanks. Likewise, 23 Punjab also fought a legendary battle against a major Pakistani armour thrust at Laungewala, where 37 Pakistani medium tanks were either destroyed or captured intact.* 18 Punjab, in freezing weather, captured the high altitude Brachil Pass in the Kargil sector of Jammu & Kashmir, while Nangi Tekri, in the Poonch sector of the same state, was captured heroically by 21 Punjab. 22 Punjab, too, earned fame by capturing Chak Amru in the Shakargarh area. The battalions of the Punjab Regiment have also excelled in combating terrorism in Punjab, Jammu & Kashmir and in the north-eastern states. Many have also participated in 'Operation Pawan' in Sri Lanka.

While the sterling post-independence performance of the various battalions have been well chronicled in a book form titled *By Land and Sea* written by Brigadier V.R. Raghavan, (later Lieutenant General, now retired), the achievements of the Regiment from 1980 till date have also been lucidly illustrated in the second volume of the regimental history book of a similar title written by Colonel Anil Shorey, (Lancers – 2002) hence this present book will only highlight the exceptionally rich history of the 300 year old battalion – 15 Punjab (Patiala).

---

* A must read for all Galleymen is the latest book *'Pakistan's Failed Gamble – The Battle of Laungewala.'* Released internationally, it has been published in 2005 by Manas Publications, 24 Ansari Road, Daryaganj New Delhi – 110 002.

2

The Inception of 1st Patiala

The origin of what is now known as 15th Battalion the Punjab Regiment (Patiala) can be traced as far back as 1705, to the very year when the State of Patiala formally came into being. It was a smaller entity before that time, formed out of a loose Sikh Confederacy and various families existing then, where the free-brothers spirit prevailed at large amongst its men as they relied mainly on booty gained in various battles for maintenance, as was the common code of conduct at that time. It will be interesting to trace the lineage of the State much before 1705.

The founder of Patiala State was born in a family of Sidhu clan. The common ancestor of the Sidhus was the Rajput Chief Jaisal, who founded the state and city of Jaisalmer. A descendant of Jaisal in the twenty-ninth generation was Phul, the son of Rupchand who lost his life in an inter-clan fight in the year 1618.

Chowdhury Phul had two sons, Triloka and Rama, who were the founders of the Phul dynasty. The subsequent Phulkian States, which included the states of Patiala, Nabha and Jind, were all offshoot of this dynasty.

It is from Chowdhury Phul's second son Rama that the Patiala family traces its lineage.

The Phul brothers had constant trouble with the fledgling but unstable Sikh Confederacy. However, they had the blessings of Guru Gobind Singh who conferred on them the honours 'Tera Ghar so Mera Ghar' which, till today, forms the coat of arms of Patiala State.

However, according to available records and popular folklores, Bakshi Lakhna Dogar was not only the organizer and self-proclaimed head of Patiala State but he also became military chief of all Phulkian forces towards the end of the 17th century. The nucleus of Patiala State Forces was actually provided by Bakshi Lakhna and his one thousand followers to include a large number of Dogra family members. This fighter kept on increasing the army by the thousands.

Bakshi Lakhna Dogar had an elder brother Ala Singh who, by right, should have been head of Patiala State. That aside, both brothers had cordial relations and used to meet regularly at the house of a saintly person at village Tapa to receive his blessings for their respective ambitious plans of conquering lands and territories. Lakhna Dogar, who was more ambitious of the two brothers, would set out with his thousands of followers regularly to conquer the territory from the banks of the Ravi river to Cis-Sutlej jungle area. He was determined to get this area, and to try his fate with the hope of chalking out some principality for himself out of the crumbling Mughal Empire. The followers of Lakhna were all warlike, -tall statured, well-built and able-bodied men ready to do or die at the orders of the head of their tribe. However, over a few years Lakhna's followers were impressed with the saintly and more capable ways and practical approach of Ala Singh, who was by then holding the title of respect - Baba. They convinced Lakhna to put in their lot with Ala Singh, who soon became their sole, rightful and undisputed leader, and adorned the mantle of 'Raja'.

The Inception of 1st Patiala

Bakshi Lakhna, while placing his hands on the sacred book of his faith, the holy Quran, swore his faithfulness and loyalty to the person of the newly proclaimed 'Raja Ala Singh', to his 'gaddi' and his descendants, and asked his master for one single boon to be granted to him and his descendants, that they be given the right to pay their respects to the throne and to repeat the same oath of loyalty at least once a year in order to commemorate the sacred day of union between himself and his master Ala Singh in 1705. Having been granted this boon, Lakhna directed all his best efforts in collecting men of good fighting qualities around Baba Ala Singh. Sardar Gurbaksh Singh Sarao, belonging to Mai Fatto's family and an inhabitant of village Tapa, soon joined alongwith his relatives and followers. Later on many tribal heads and influential men belonging to different Jat tribes of the surrounding areas declared themselves as the subjects of Baba Ala Singh, who had earlier openly announced that all tillers of the soil in his state would be treated as peasant proprietors, and not as tenants. The base of Baba Ala Singh at that time, to include that of his army, was village Longowal.

From the time of coming of Ala Singh into political prominence, all the Phulkian chiefs followed the rulers of Patiala in all their subsequent expeditions of territorial conquests.

3
The Maturing

By 1722 the Patiala army was conceived as a full-fledged and cohesive fighting unit by Baba Ala Singh, the rightful founder of Patiala State. It was given concrete shape by one Bakshi Ganda Singh, who was in a way the first commander in chief. Although no name or designation was assigned to the new unit, yet it was a unique fighting force in those days, as very few regular units existed in any of the Indian States, and the East India Company was non-existent then.

For all historical and practical purposes, roughly from this time onwards begins the period of regular conquests, territorial possessions, levying and collection of land revenue, protection of conquered subjects, peace with powerful neighbours, administration of justice, and disbursement of regular payment to the soldiers and men in service.

Baba Ala Singh established himself at Barnala in 1723 after defeating its chieftain in a battle. For the next three decades he, having overwhelmed most of the opposing Sikh chieftains, built up a sizeable force of 7000 horsemen and a similar number of foot soldiers. In all the battles fought by the Patialas, victory was assured and certain, but

The Maturing

the finest moment of glory attained at that time was during the Bhatti Wars fought in 1738. However, a brief setback took place in 1748 when Ahmed Shah Durrani, a Afghan Chieftain, at the instance of the Governor of Sirhind, defeated Baba Ala Singh and his allies. However, subsequently in 1751 the Afghan ruler, as a humane gesture, presented Baba Ala Singh a Robe of Honour and conferred on him the title of Raja, as also allowed the Baba to retain all villages and territories under his control before returning to Afghanistan. Baba Ala Singh now became an acclaimed leader of this all-triumphant Dera Formataion, and, in the next few years he brought areas of Pinjore, captured in 1768, to Tohana, captured in 1769, under his control.

Immediately after the Afghan Chieftain returned to his country, Baba Ala Singh shifted his capital from Barnala to Patiala in 1752, and soon after constructed the Patiala Fort. He also constructed about a dozen smaller fortifications and outposts all along the boundary of the state to ensure safety of the people inhabiting the state. Furthermore, these outposts also gave time for the main force to get ready to meet any threat from any direction. It can be said that Patiala State was firmly established and its subjects lived peacefully. Soon after that Baba Ala Singh decided to deal severely with Zain Khan, the Governor of Sirhind for siding with the Afghan Chieftain Durrani. For this campaign the forces of other Phulkian Chiefs and those of the various Cis-Sutlej Sikhs also joined up with the Patiala forces.

The opportunity came in December 1763 when Zain Khan, after filling his coffers from tax collection, was returning from Rajpura to Sirhind. Baba Ala Singh engaged Zain Khan in a battle a few miles from Ambala, defeated and killed him. Sirhind fell to him in early 1764. Baba Ala Singh, during all these operations, showed daring, dash and outstanding leadership qualities, a tradition that pervaded his successors. Patiala Army, during the remaining part of the century, continued to grow and develop into a firm, well-knit armed group. It could take to the field at any time against any army in a disciplined way.

The successor and grandson of Baba Ala Singh, Maharaja Amar Singh continued the military traditions and during his short reign, fought and defeated the Nawab of Malerkotla in 1767, seizing important territory from him. Pinjore was taken in 1768. He also took Bathinda and killed its Chieftain, Jodha Singh, in 1771. Saifabad was captured the same year. He defeated the belligerent Bhatti Chiefs and extended his territories to Sirsa and Fatehabad, while his Dewan, Manu Mal, defeated the Governor of Hansi and overran Hansi and Hissar, which were later retaken by the British. Thus, by the turn of the century, Patiala emerged as the most powerful state between the Sutlej and the Jamuna. This first regular army unit played a very important role in laying, extending and consolidating the boundaries of the state of Patiala, and its legendary name spread far and wide throughout India.

4

New Shape and Conquests

The re-modelling of the battalion, based on the French infantry battalion model, took place on 13 April 1783, Baisakhi day by the Indian calendar. A certain Ghani Beg of Lucknow was ordered to raise this regular model unit by Maharani Hukum Kaur, mother of Maharaja Sahib Singh, who was just a minor at that time. No name or designation was given to this striking unit. From 1783 to 1823 it was commanded by a certain Gazi Beg whose rank was known as 'Kumaidan', French for Commandant, in consonance with the French rank structure. As per records, during the period 1805 and 1855, the Patiala army was being trained by French army instructors, since the Royal family of Patiala had developed extremely cordial relations with the French government. It was amongst the very few army units in India to be trained by the French before the British influence could spread through Central India. Therefore, the first three commandants of the 1st Patiala infantry, that is Gazi Beg, Dharam Singh and Gajjan Singh, earned the title of 'Kumaidan'.

During the second year of Kumaidan Gazi Beg's tenure the unit successfully fought against the Maratthas in 1784, and came into further prominence through its valour, agility and uncanny minor tactics.

Legend has it that during this war the superior Marattha force was challenged and defeated by the Patiala Army under the temporary command of a royal lady, proving that the ladies of the House of Patiala during those days had taken on to soldiering, and were no less in valour than their male counterparts. When His Highness Maharaja Sahib Singh was still a minor, his elder sister Bibi Sahib Kaur's daring skirmishes with the Maratthas was another such example.

Prior to this war the Maratthas, having dealt ruthlessly with the Moghal rulers, crossed the Jamuna early in 1784 and set their eyes on Punjab, particularly Patiala. At that time the Patiala rule was facing acute domestic problems. The situation further deteriorated as a result a strike instigated by a dismissed and disgruntled Dewan of Patiala Darbar named Nand Mal. He soon invited the Scindias of Gwalior to annex Patiala. This invitation was accepted, and as the Maratthas advanced towards Punjab, they brushed away minor chieftains enroute. In mid-1784, at Mubarakpur near Ambala, the legendary Bibi Sahib Kaur of Patiala came out of her chariot, brandishing her sword at the advancing Maratthas. While doing so she motivated the Sikh soldiers through exhortations, saying that it would be a terrible shame for the Sikhs to show signs of weakness during such times of crisis. On seeing the royal lady leading the attack from the front line, the Sikh soldiers, during their subsequent attacks, fought the war with renewed fury and vigour and the situation was temporarily stabilised. Bibi Sahib Kaur then planned to attack the Maratthas next morning, just before daybreak. But before this attack could take place, the Patiala force surprised the Maratthas and Bibi Sahib Kaur as well by causing confusion amongst the Marattha rank and file through spreading rumours, leading to much chaos and demoralization in their camp.

New Shape and Conquests

The rumours were that a large, highly motivated and well armed Sikh force was immediately about to join the Patialas fighting the Maratthas. Under the erroneous impression through such rumours, the demoralized Maratthas withdrew hastily, fighting only a weak rearguard action. This was a magnificent victory for the Patialas, that too under the leadership of a lady. A solid tradition was thus built - that of never to withdraw even when against a vastly superior force.

In 1809 the British declared suzerainty in Cis-Sutlej area. The Patiala Chiefs maintained cordial relations and avoided any collision with the British. They also did not meddle around with the affairs of the feuding chiefs across Sutlej River. Patiala State accepted British protection and promised to help them when needed in return.

The Patialas participated in the Gorkha War of 1814 when General Amar Singh Thapa, an adventurist from Nepal, occupied the British protected independent hill states and a fairly large portion of what is now the state of UP. Infuriated, the British Government of India soon declared war against the Gurkhas. Colonel Ochterlonly (later who received the title of Lord) led a column of British troops, with the Patialas forming part of his force to the hill states from Ropar. Raja Karam Singh, the Maharaja of Patiala at that time, had sent his infantry to participate in this campaign on the request of the British. He had also sent his cavalry to guard the foothills.

After the capture of Nalagarh and Taragarh, the British forces defeated General Thapa in April 1814, but later they permitted him to retire alongwith his forces after taking a firm commitment of abstaining from such misadventures in future. Colonel Ochterlonly had this to say about the Patialas in his special dispatch: - "The physique, discipline and fighting qualities of Patiala soldiers who fought alongwith the British troops was commendable". For his services, Raja Karam Singh was awarded a portion of Bhagat (now known as Solan), including Simla and Keonthal, to include Chail. The military tradition of Patiala soldiery was now fully established. In later years Chail became the summer capital of Patiala State.

It was only in 1819 that the designation of 1st Infantry was given to the unit. This was done so because Maharaja Karam Singh had ordered the raising of five more Infantry units, three additional cavalry regiments and a few more regular horsed artillery units.

In 1823 Kumaidan Dharam Singh took over the command of 1st Infantry. No major operation was conducted during his period of command from 1823 to 1842. However, the 1st Infantry under his command, and thereafter under the command of Kumaidan Gajjan Singh, who took over the reins of the battalion in 1843, played a major role in raising and training the additional infantry battalions which came into the fold of Patiala army.

During the Kaithal Rebellion of 1843, the Patiala State sent some 2000 cavalry, an equal number of infantry and some artillery to help the British troops. The rebel leader Tek Singh was taken prisoner. Here again the Patiala contingent proved its uncanny fighting qualities, which were highly appreciated by the Commissioner at Ambala in his dispatch to higher authorities.

Under Kumaidan Gajjan Singh the battalion fought the Sutlej War, which was also known as the First Sikh War of 1845-47.

On 23 December 1845, on the death of Raja Karam Singh of Patiala, his 21 years old son Narinder Singh

New Shape and Conquests

succeeded him. The new ruler also offered his full support to the British. At the time of the Second Sikh War he loaned Rs 30 lakhs to the British, besides other material support.

The unit thereafter fought against George Thomas, the self - proclaimed Chief of Hansi, at Lajwana in 1854.

The battalion's command passed into the hands of Kumaidan Amir Khan in 1856. It may be noted that by this time the French army instructors were no longer retained by Patiala state, and all training aspects within the Patiala army were being looked after under the aegis of the commandant of 1st Patiala. The title of Kumaidan, too, was formally done away with during the time Amir Khan's command entered its second decade. However, Amir Khan continued to use the title till 1873, by when the last of the French instructors left Patiala state for their homeland.

One of the reasons attributed to relinquishing the services of French instructors by Patiala State was that the influence of British Indian army had spread practically throughout India; and, due to a state of near war between Britain and France, the former requested the Maharaja of Patiala for dispensing with their services. In return the British offered their own instructors to the Maharaja of Patiala. Their latter request, however, was not accepted by the Patiala royalty. They felt, quite rightfully, that their army was well trained and did not require the services of any foreign army instructors any more.

Under Colonel Amir Khan the unit played a very important part in maintaining peace and security over a wide area during the violent and turbulent days of 1857, the days of the so called Indian Mutiny. Thereafter, the Maharaja sent his best troops under the ablest military leaders to numerous flashpoints such as Ferozepur, Jhajar, Karnal, Rohtak, Hansi, Hissar, Delhi and Dholpur, enabling the British troops to meet the challenge effectively. Sardar Partap Singh and Khalifa Mohammad Hasan, the Prime Minister of the State, distinguished themselves during the siege of Delhi. That apart, Kanwar Dip Singh distinguished himself at Thanesar; Sardar Hazure Singh and Hira Singh at Ambala; Sardar Karan Singh and Kahan Singh at Hissar; Sardar Dal Singh and Fateh Singh at Hansi and Sardar Jeevan Singh at Ferozepur. All British commanders held Patiala commanders and men in very high esteem.

Around this time a valuable contribution was made by the Patialas at Dholpur, where the rebels of Dholpur, after getting control of Gwalior, invested Dholpur. The Raja lost complete control of his State, and the fugitive ruler of Scindia also fled for safety to Dholpur. The Maharaja of Patiala's troops retrieved the state and escorted Maharaja Scindia back to Gwalior. This in turn enabled the British troops to defeat the rebels at Agra. Thereafter, at the request of the Commissioner, some 1200 Patiala troops were sent to Jhajar where the Nawab had revolted and joined hands with Delhi rebels. The splendid support provided by the Maharaja of Patiala was suitably rewarded by the British. Narnaul, Kanauj and Kamaron were awarded by the British to Patiala State in perpetual sovereignty.

Sir Douglas Forsyth, the Commissioner of Cis-Sutlej states at Ambala, had this to say in his dispatch to the Governor General:- "The straightforward and loyal conduct of cis-Sutlej states was of infinite importance to our cause at that time. The Maharaja of Patiala (Narinder Singh) was an orthodox Hindu whose position and career alike commanded respect. His support at such a crisis was worth a Brigade of English troops." Such was the reputation of the Patialas that made its subjects proud indeed. However, Maharaja Narinder Singh passed away in November 1867 and his only son Mohinder was acclaimed to the throne.

New Shape and Conquests

On his death in 1876, his son Rajinder, who was then just four years old, inherited the kingdom of Patiala.

By this time India Office, through a memorandum, allowed the Patiala Army's strength to be retained as under:-

Regular Troops

Cavalry	-	2032
Infantry	-	3020
Artillery* Crew	-	238
Total		5290

Irregulars

Cavalry	-	411
Infantry	-	1381
Grand Total		7082

* **Note**: 20 Artillery guns were horse drawn. The remainder were based on bullock pack.

The Patialas thereafter played a prominent role in the Mohmand Expedition and also at Malakand in 1897. In August that year 1st Patiala was sent for the relief of British troops entrapped at Shabkadar, north of Peshawar. It came under Mohmand Field Force. Due to its effective domination of the area, Afridi tribesmen were not permitted to move around freely in the area held by the Patialas. By September the tribesmen were totally overwhelmed and asked for peace thereafter. The Frontier areas soon became subdued and the Patialas then moved for the relief of Malakand through river Swat.

The Patialas had their first baptism of fire in the Malakand. The Maharaja of Patiala offered the services of

1st Patiala and a battery each of artillery and cavalry to the Malakand Field Force. The Battalion Group proved its mettle in the Swat valley and areas adjacent to the Black Mountains. Later on 1st Patiala took an active part in the Tirah Expedition as well. Due to heavy demand of regular and State Force troops, another battalion of the Patiala forces, that is 2nd Patiala, was also inducted into this region and acquitted itself creditably in all these operations. The Maharaja himself, at just 25 years of age then, served on the staff in these operations, and, at the conclusion of the operations, was thanked by the Imperial Government for his services, and the award of the G.C.S.I. (Grand Cross for Services in India) was conferred upon him, which is most creditable.

On return after the Tirah operation of the two Patiala battalions to Patiala State, Maharaja Rajinder Singh ordered the provision of various cantonment facilities and construction of proper accommodation for his troops in Patiala. However, it was during this period that the unit was re-designated to 1st Patiala Imperial Service Infantry (Rajindra Sikh) in May 1900. His Highness died suddenly on November 8, 1900, when only twenty eight years of age. Maharaja Rajinder Singh was held in the highest esteem throughout India as a generous and hospitable ruler. His successor was Maharaja Bhupinder Singh, who was just ten years old when his father died.

From 1902 onwards the Patiala units once again re-organised, equipped and trained on the Indian Pattern of War Establishment. Two full sized units – 1 Rajindra Sikh Infantry and 1 Patiala Lancers, as part of Imperial Service Troops, were kept in a state of readiness to take to field at short notice, as and when required by the British government.

New Shape and Conquests

For better coordination between the various state governments and the British government in India, the latter nominated civil servants to function as Political Agents. One Political Agent was therefore accredited to each independent Indian state. Similarly, during operations on the military plane, one British Indian Army officer was also accredited to each state. He had two or more Special Service Officers (SSOs) placed under him who would ensure proper implementation of operational training and equipment policy directives emanated from the War Office/Army Headquarters from time to time.

His Highness the Maharaja Bhupinder Singh assured his troops at Patiala that suitable arrangements had been made to look after the dependents of all ranks, and exhorted them to fight loyally and bravely in all the battles of the King Emperor, whenever and wherever they might be sent. Revised monetary scales and allowances were also spelt out. These assurances had a telling effect on the troops, as subsequent years would prove.

5

1st Patiala During World War I

Throughout the late 19th and early 20th century, the European pot had been simmering due to border disputes as well as historical and ethnic rivalries. The assassination by Serbs of Archduke Francis Ferdinand of Austria, the heir to the Austrian throne, and his wife on 28 June 1914 at Sarajevo finally sparked the long conflict that became famous as World War I, or the 'Great War'. Though it had no treaties to uphold, Britain decided to send its British Expeditionary Force (BEF) and joined the war on 4 August 1914.

The Great War began in August 1914 when seven German armies, totalling a million and a half men, swept in swarms through the Belgian plains hinging around Verdun. Germany had planned to pulverize France by concentrating almost its entire field army in the west, and then turn east to defeat the Russians. Britain sent its BEF consisting of two corps of four (later six) infantry divisions, including the Indian Corps. By October 1914, both sides dug lines of trenches from the North Sea to the Swiss frontier. The war had become truly static, and expertise in trench warfare was mandatory to ensure success in battle. The Indian troops who were sent to France, even though

1st Patiala During World War I

having vast experience of fighting in the frontiers, were ill-organised, ill-armed and ill-trained to fight the Germans in this static form of warfare—and the cold and wet conditions of Europe. However, various commanders praised them for their discipline, valour and ferocious fighting abilities.

Even when the British government in India was contemplating to send a large contingent to France in 1914, the maintenance of peace in the North-West Frontier of India still remained its chief concern. It was after considerable deliberation that the government decided to send its forces to France and the Middle East after leaving the minimum essential troops in the North-West Frontier Province (NWFP) to tackle the rebelling tribes in that region. With this decision, an opportunity came for overseas service for the Patiala forces as well, and two of its units i.e. 1st Rajindra Sikh Infantry and 1st Patiala Lancers were mobilized. The troops concentrated at Bombay by late September to sail for the Middle East and Suez Canal area for operations against the Turkish Army, which had joined the Axis Powers by then. The Maharaja also left Patiala for the front with his two units on 5 October 1914. Having sailed with them across the Indian Ocean, on reaching Aden he was taken seriously ill with nephritis, and the medical verdict was that he must return to India, which he did!

The battalion, under the command of Colonel Gurbux Singh Jeji Bahadur (1912-17), with Captain G.S.F. Routh as Senior Special Service Officer and Captain H Campbell as Special Service Officer, was brigaded with the 32 Imperial Service Brigade and incorporated with the 11 Infantry Division under the command of Major General A.W. Wallace, CB. The unit arrived at Suez via Aden on November 16, and at Ismailia five days later.

After some initial training, the battalion was sent to Port Said for duty on the Suez Canal, and it defended the portion of the Canal from Tinch to Port Said during the Turkish attacks on the canal between January and February 1915. On 22 March 1915 a detachment of the battalion took over an armoured train and proceeded to Abu Halab in order to join the defences against an attack by the Turks on El – Kubri. In July and September 1915, a company each of the battalion and 1st Patiala Lancers reinforced 14 Sikh at Dardanelles and Gallipoli respectively, while the rest of 1 Patiala Lancers moved to Mesopotamia. Their performance in these new theatres were legendary, to say the least.

On returning to India on the advice of medical specialists, the Maharaja of Patiala's health soon improved and, realizing that the need of the hour was the supply of recruits, both to keep up and augment the Indian contingents, set to the task personally with characteristic zest and earnestness. The first step he took in this direction was to tour his state from 21 January to 6 March 1915. He also held recruiting 'darbars' at the principal centres and exhorted his people and officials to do their utmost to provide manpower. This personal appeal had a great effect. Recruitment was actively pursued, and by the end of 1917 no less than 10, 270 Patiala subjects were confirmed as serving in the Indian army. The figure was larger than that of all the other Punjab states taken together, and many other subjects of His Highness, living or sojourning at the time outside the state, also joined the Indian Army. Simultaneously recruits were being enlisted for the Maharaja's own contingent of Imperial Service Troops, including eight companies of Patiala Infantry, four squadrons of Imperial Service Lancers, two new squadrons consisting 300 ranks, one machine gun section, two Mule Corps and a Camel Corps. The 72nd Hired Camel Corps was raised by His Highness at the beginning of 1916, and altogether

1st Patiala During World War I

a total of 4,307 men, comprising 2,933 Infantry, 1,230 Mule and Camel Corps, and 144 Hired Camel Corps were recruited for these units. This made the total enlistment of Patiala men towards the end of 1917 no less than 14, 576.

Coming back to the war front, from March to the middle of September 1915 the rest of 1st Patiala remained on the Suez Canal defence duty from Ferry Post, Ismailia, to Serapeum. Thereafter, till early 1916 it was based at Zagazig. On April 22 1916, two companies of the battalion formed part of the Mitla Pass Mobile Column under 60 Infantry Division in Jordon Valley to reconnoitre enemy territory on foot. This mission was extremely arduous owing to excessive heat and scarcity of water, yet not a single man fell out. On September 13 one of the two companies formed part of the mobile column to reconnoitre the enemy area in the direction of Bir-Abu-Tif and Abu Garad. From the beginning of 1916 to the middle of April 1917 the entire battalion was placed under 60 Infantry Division and remained on front line duty on various posts in Jordan, stretching from Kubri to Ayun Mussa, including Gabel Murr Post and Bir-Mubiauk. It also saw action with the famous Maghdeba Column which operated in the Jordan Valley. From the middle of April to the end of September 1917 the battalion remained on the Palestine front where it carried out lines of communication protection duties.

The second anniversary of the war was celebrated at Patiala, where Sikh leaders from all over the country flocked, the call having come to them from the head of the community. The Punjab Government was specially represented by the Political Agent to the Phulkian States. The Maharaja made a memorable speech which received wide publicity in which he related the duties performed by the Patialas during the hour of world crisis, to the teachings of the great Guru, who conferred the primacy of the community upon the ruler of Patiala. He proudly recalled the fact that the Guru, who called the Phulkian House his own house, also blessed the English nation for saving India from the clutches of misrule and tyranny. "I need hardly mention that all my regular Imperial Service Troops are serving at the front, and are being maintained by me at full strength. You will be glad to know that, of the Indian States, Patiala stands first in the number of combatants supplied to the armed forces," he said.

During mid-September 1917 Colonel Ishwar Singh Bahadur, OBI, took over the command of 1st Patiala. On 27 September 1917 the battalion was sent to Mandur for duty on the firing line, and was incorporated with 21 Army Corps. On 1 November it dug trenches near Baiket Abu-Melik and then occupied them to defend Tel-el-Jenmi and Wadi Ghuzzee against a diversionary attack by the Turks. After the capture of Gaza-Bir Shabha line, the battalion was employed on lines of communication duties for about four months.

Back home at Patiala, on a special recruitment drive organized by the Maharaja of Patiala on the occasion of the third anniversary of the Great War, His Highness reiterated – "The Punjab tops the list of all the provinces of India in the recruitment of combatants for the front, and Patiala holds similar honour amongst the Indian states." Then he said the golden words – " We cannot boast of having millionaires amongst us, although, in spite of this drawback, our province, small as it is, stands only next to the Bombay and Bengal Presidencies in subscribing to the War Loan". He went on to say:- "Much as we believe in the power of matter and science, we believe still more firmly in the powers of the spirit and the spiritual agencies working unseen under the direction of the Akal Purukh. The Tenth Guru has said, I quote: -

1st Patiala During World War I

"O Sun, O Moon, O Ocean of mercy,
Listen to my prayers now.
I do not beg anything else of Thee,
Only grant the desire of my heart
To die fighting with arms
In the thick of battle, this shall
Be my gratification
Thou supporter of devotees, the eternal
Mother of the universe,
Grant me this boon through thy grace divine".

He again said – "Let the Khalsa, therefore, take the inspiration from this sacred 'Wak' of our Guru, and to go forth cheerfully and full of faith to fight for their 'King and Country".

On 14 April 1918, First Patiala took over firing line duty at Auja, and subsequently at the Choraniye Bridge - head defences, and was incorporated in the Desert Mounted Corps under the command of Lieutenant General Sir H.G. Chauvol, KC, MG, KCB, from 27 April to 5 May. The battalion took part in the second Es-Salt operations, storming the positions at Kabar Masjid Kajahir and on the hills near El-Houd. It remained on firing line duty in Jordan Valley until the end of September. From 23 September to 10 October, the First Patiala formed part of 'Chaytor's Force' for active operations and was present in the last advance and attack on Es-Salt and Amman. The General Staff Officer to the General Officer Commanding (GOC) of the Chaytor's Force wrote to the Commanding Officer 1st Patiala thus - "The C-in-C desires me to thank you for the excellent work and courage which culminated in the surrender to entire Turkish Force south of Amman".

GOC 'Chaytor's Force' had also the following to say through his Chief of Staff vide his letter No 92 dated 30

September 1918, which was addressed to Patiala Imperial Service Infantry, - "The GOC desires me to convey to you his congratulations and thanks for the excellent work, which culminated in the surrender of the entire Turkish Force south of Amman. In doing so, I wish to thank all ranks of this force for their splendid endurance and loyal co-operation, and to congratulate them on the success which they have achieved by their courage and determination".

The Brigade Major of 20 Indian Infantry Brigade, vide his letter dated 12 May 1918 addressed to SSO, Alwar Imperial Service Infantry, SSO Gwalior Imperial Infantry and SSO Patiala Imperial Service Infantry, said: "The General Officer Commanding has much pleasure in communicating the following:

"Major General J.S.M. Shea, CB, CMG, DSC, Commanding 60 Division has written to the GOC Brigade saying that he very much hoped, before leaving the Jordan Valley, to have had the opportunity of thanking the Brigade for all the help they gave him while under his command during the recent operations. The good work they did was carried out under trying and difficult conditions. Major General Shea particularly wishes to thank the Patiala Imperial Service Infantry for their fine work and wishes GOC Brigade to tell them that he greatly appreciated their efforts. Lieutenant General Sir H.G. Chauvol, KCB, KCMG, Commanding Desert Mounted Corps, has also expressed his appreciation of the good work done by the Brigade."

Commander 32 Imperial Service Infantry, vide his letter dated 6 July 1915 addressed to SSO Patiala Imperial Service Infantry, says:

"Please ask Colonel Gurbaksh Singh to publish the following in Battalion Orders – viz—The GOC 32 Imperial Service Brigade has much pleasure in informing the 'Rajindra Sikhs' that the 'Honour' of sending a Double Company to join Sikhs, now fighting in the Gallipoli peninsula, has been accorded to the Regiment. In congratulating the Regiment most heartily in this Honour, the GOC wishes that the best of luck may attend this Double Company and feels sure that it will bring honour and glory both to the good name of the Sikh brotherhood, to that of the Regiment and to that of Imperial Service Troops in general. The GOC has also been much pleased with the good conduct and work of the Regiment since its arrival in Egypt and trusts that an opportunity may occur later of giving HH the Maharaja of Patiala's 'Rajindra Sikh' a more prominent part of the Great War".

The zest and ardour with which the Imperial Service contingents, and other subjects of His Highness who served in the war, was well rewarded by the single honour conferred upon him by his selection to attend the Imperial War Conference and Imperial War Cabinet in London in 1918 as the representative of the ruling princes of India. The first selection of the kind was made in the previous year when his close friend, His Highness the Maharaja of Bikaner, attended the same.

At a farewell banquet on the eve of the departure of the Maharaja from Patiala, Mr M.L. Crump, the Political Agent of the Phulkian States, proposed the health of His Highness whom he congratulated as the head of the premier Sikh State, and on the number of the Sikhs serving in the Indian Army being nearly equal to one in three of their men of military age, and that the Sikhs had won half of the honours and decorations awarded.

His Highness left Bombay on May 21, 1918, and, taking the Italian overland route, arrived in London on June 12. He was immediately promoted through a Royal Warrant to the rank of Major General, and was appointed Honorary Colonel of the 15th Ludhiana Sikhs – a regiment containing many Patiala men, and which so distinguished itself in the relief of the French Cavalry at La Bassee early in the war; as also in the battles of Givenchy, Neuve Chapelle and Festubert, and in the second battle of Ypres. Subsequently, in 1919, His Highness was appointed Colonel-in-Chief of the newly raised 1/140th (Patiala) Infantry.

The Maharaja was regular and assiduous in his attendance at the sessions of the War Conference and the War Cabinet. He lunched with their Majesties the King and Queen at Buckingham Palace on June 20, 1918, and was afterwards invested with the insignia of Knight Grand Cross of the Order of the British Empire, a dignity, which had already been conferred as a New Year Honour on January 1. A fortnight later the Maharaja paid a brief visit to the Belgian front. He was invited by the King of Belgium to meet him, but illness prevented his accepting the invitation.

Immediately after the Imperial War Conference, the Maharaja indulged in his long cherished desire to visit the various fronts before his return to India. He first made a tour of the Western front, including a special pilgrimage to La Bassee, where the 15th Sikhs alongwith some of his own troops fought splendidly soon after arriving at the battle front in 1914. While proceeding to Egypt, His Highness went to the Palestine front where his troops were being employed on firing line duty in the Jordan valley. The Maharaja joined them there on August 17, accompanied by the Commander-in-Chief of the Egyptian Expeditionary Force, Field Marshal Lord Allenby, who was all praises for Patiala troops. The Patiala troops were

1st Patiala During World War I

naturally greatly delighted to be visited by their Commander-in-Chief, and received the personal thanks to Lord Allenby for the excellent work done during the operations. Before His Highness left Egypt, the Sultan conferred upon him the Grand Cross of the Order of Nile. The visit, coming at a time when the tide of war had distinctly turned in the Near Eastern theatres of war, attracted some attention in the newspapers and many photographs appeared of His Highness, busy on informal inspection work at the front. Thereafter, the Maharaja left for India. He reached Patiala on 6 September 1918, receiving a great ovation from his people. He left the same evening for Chail, the summer capital of the State, and on September 18 paid a visit to the Viceroy at Simla to narrate to him the proceedings at the Imperial War Conference held in London.

On 10 October 1918, First Patiala proceeded on a route march from Amman to Gaza and from Gaza reached Suez via Kantara on 8 January 1919. On the following day the battalion embarked at Suez to return home, and arrived at Karachi on 24 October 1919. It reached Patiala on 27 January 1919, after more than four years of active service overseas.

The Patiala contingents' return to Patiala coincided with the Lieutenant Governor of Punjab's visit to the State. He reviewed a very smart parade of the troops on 23 February 1919. On behalf of the British Government he congratulated them on their return home and appreciated their military services rendered to India and the Empire. In the course of his speech, he gave an admirable summary of the achievements of the Maharaja's forces:

"The Patiala Imperial Service Troops were among the first to take to the field against the enemy, and you did not leave it till the enemy were completely crushed. You have worthily upheld the splendid traditions of the Patiala State and the Sikh stage, and their services in Mesopotamia earned the commendation of Generals Maude and Marshall".

The following is a copy of an extract from the War Diary of a company of 14 Sikh dated 22 August 1915 at Dardanelles: - "Patiala company did very well this day under Subedar Kahla Singh. They were on an exposed flank alongwith a few of 14 Sikh, and stood firm when other troops in the line were taken back by the remnants of another battalion, which retired through the line after they had been cut up and failed in an attack, losing 500 out of 800".

The total casualties of the battalion during World War I were as follows:-

	Officers	Men	Total
(a) At the Dardanelles			
Killed in action	1	16	17
Died of wounds	-	8	8
Injured	6	105	111
Missing	-	1	1
Total	7	130	137
(b) In Egypt and Palestine			
Killed in action	-	5	5
Died of wounds	-	9	9
Injured	-	82	82
Died of accident	-	1	1
Wounded by accident	1	1	2
Total	1	98	99
Grand Total	8	228	236

1st Patiala During World War I

The sum of the casualties incurred by the battalion at Dardanelles, Egypt and in Palestine, to include in killed, wounded and missing were 8 officers and 228 men, of whom 39 were killed in enemy action.

A total of 54 honours and awards were awarded to First Patiala during the War, to include one Military Cross (MC); four Indian Order to Merit (IOM); five Order to British India Second Class (OBI – II); eight Indian Distinguished Service Medal (IDSM); 21 Mentioned-in-Despatches (MDs); ten Indian Meritorious Service Medal (IMSM); one Order of King George (with Sword) First Class; one Order of King George (with Sword) Fourth Class; one Serbian Gold Medal; one Serbian Silver Medal and one Order of the Nile Fourth Class.

The Total strength that formed and kept up this battalion in field included 18 mounted officers, 28 other officers, 1599 men, 184 followers (akin to non combatants enrolled), 16 horses and 77 mules.

DURING THE GREAT WAR 1914-18

His Highness Maharaja Bhupinder Singh leaving for the Middle East front from Apollo Bunder, Bombay, October 1914

Embarkation of 1st Patiala troops, Bombay Docks, October 1914

1st Patiala Infantry Officers riding on Patiala Lancer horses through the ruined city of Gaza - 1914

Proud 1st Patiala Machine Gunners posing for a photograph in Ismailia - 1915

Colonel Gurbax Singh Jeji Bahadur, OBI, inspecting troops of 1st Patiala at the Serapeum defences, just before the Turkish attack - 1915

1st Patiala troops wounded in the Gaza front boarding a train for further medical treatment at Cairo Military Hospital -1915

1st Patiala troops occupying dugout trenches in Jordon valley

Soldiers of 1st Patiala, who were wounded at Dardanelles, recuperating at Alexandria Military Hospital - December 1915

Soldiers of 1st Patiala, who were wounded at the Suez
and Gaza fronts, recuperating at
Cairo Military Hospital - December 1915

1st Patiala troops guarding the strategic
Jerusalem bridge - 1916

1st Patiala troops at Ferry Post defences, east of
Ismailia, Suez Canal - 1916

A mobile column of 1st Patiala camped in bivouacs,
15 miles east of the Suez Canal

1st Patiala Infantry celebrating His Highness's birthday at camp Moascar, Ismailia, to which Major General Sir A W Wallace, 11 Divisional Commander, was invited - November 1916

Captain Gurdial Singh Harika of 1st Patiala on completing his maiden operational flight after the battle at Gaza-1916

A company of 1st Patiala, on return from the Dardanelles front, disembarking in Egypt for joining the unit

1st Patiala unit at Gabel Murr camp from where they went with Maghdeba Column for operations - 1917

1st Patiala camp at Mitla valley

Troops of 1st Patiala alongwith Dogra troops during an advance to Elnot

1st Patiala camp in Jordan valley

A 1st Patiala officer amidst 35 captured Turkish guns after the attack on Gaza - Bir Shabha Line - November 1917

Captain Bhagwan Singh (left), Lieutenant Bhagwan Singh (centre) and Captain Gurdial Singh Harika sitting on a captured Turkish tank after the attack in Gaza on 2 November 1917

His Highness the Maharaja Bhupinder Singh travelling with General Birdwood (later Lord Birdwood, C-in-C India), GOC 5 Army Corps, to survey the battlefield in the European front

His Highness the Maharaja of Patiala inspecting captured German-Turco rifles at Jerusalem -August 1918

Turkish prisoners captured by 1st Patiala during their advance to Jerusalem -1918

Legendary Havildar Natha Singh of 1st Patiala establishes a record by loading 105 cartridges in one minute in Jerusalem during 1918

Officers and SSO of 1st Patiala Infantry with
His Highness and staff at Jerusalem - August 1918

Maharaja Bhupinder Singh with Field Marshal Lord Allenby
during their visit to 1st Patiala at Jerusalem - August 1918

1st Patiala disembarking at Karachi port in
February 1919, after 4 ½ years of war
service in the middle east

His Highness with General Handley inspecting troops
of 1st Patiala at Bhatinda during the
Punjab disturbances- March 1919

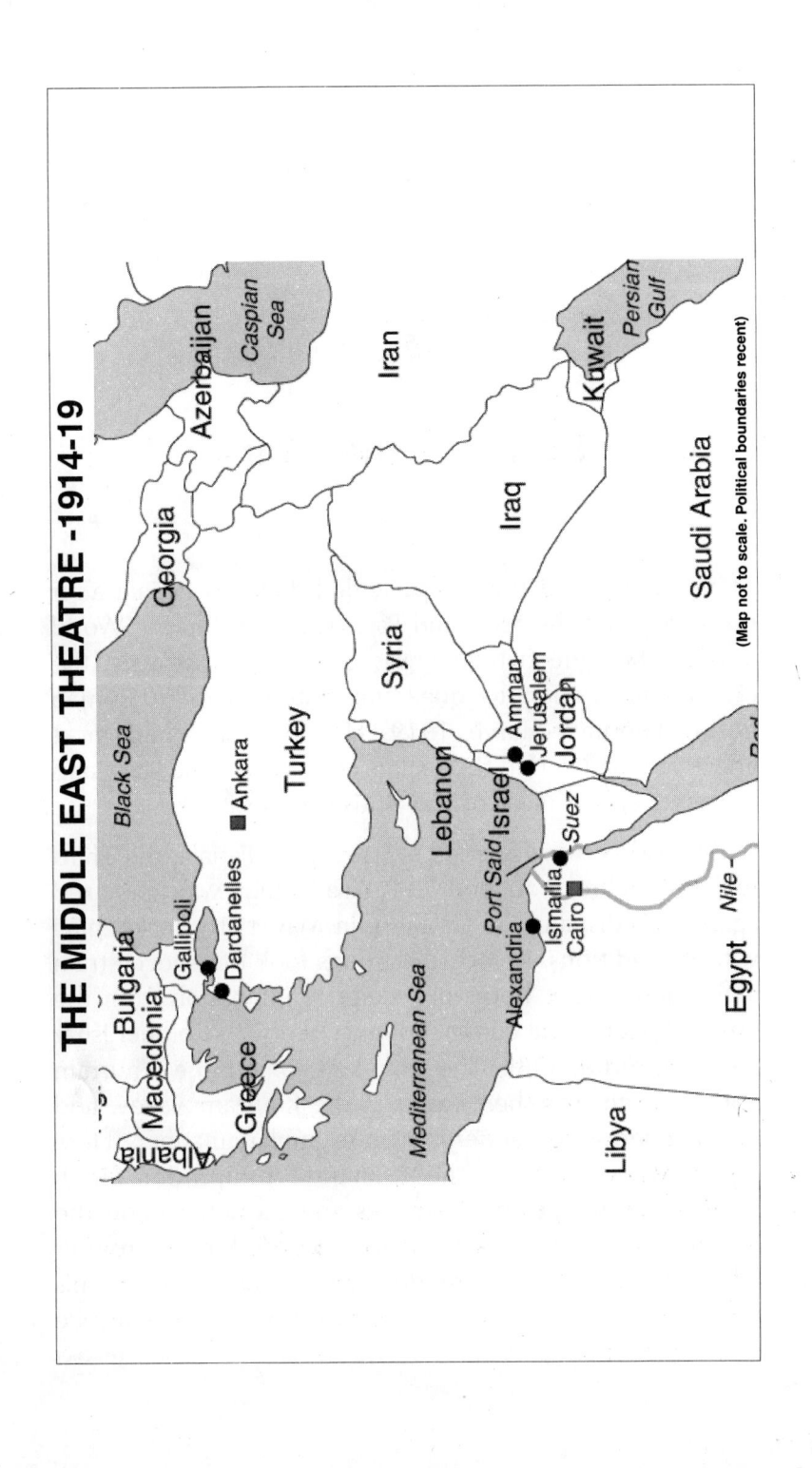

THE MIDDLE EAST THEATRE -1914-19

(Map not to scale. Political boundaries recent)

6

Between the Wars

No sooner had the troops settled down in Patiala after returning from the Suez and Palestine fronts during World War I, when the battalion was called upon to assist the civil administration to quell the disturbances in Punjab during February-March 1919. Here it functioned most effectively and within the realms of great maturity, tact and restraint, unlike most of the British troops.

As soon as they returned to barracks in Patiala, the Third Afghan War broke out and 1st Patiala Infantry was mobilized again with dispatch and alacrity in May 1919, in keeping with its traditions. In fact, the troops took the special train within just twelve hours of receipt of intimation from the Political Agent. The command remained with Colonel Ishar Singh Bahadur, OBI. The battalion joined the Khurram Force, which was then based at the Khurram Valley, and the unit performed under it in an exemplary manner. Here again Major General the Maharaja Bhupinder Singh volunteered his personal services and prevailed upon the Viceroy to accept them. He then proceeded to the frontier where he was able to render valuable assistance to his units, and returned with the battalion when an armistice was signed by the Amir.

Between the Wars

A year after returning to Patiala from the Afghan front in October 1919, the Patiala Armed Forces received orders to be placed under the Indian State Forces War Establishment Interim Scheme of 1920, with a strength of 562 all ranks, and was accordingly put through the reorganization programme.

In 1922, as a result of a major reorganization of the entire Indian Army, the unit was categorized as a Field Service Unit of Indian State Force. It was consequently formally designated as First Patiala Rajindra Sikh Infantry. The same year the command of the unit devolved on Colonel (later Lieutenant General) Gurdial Singh Harika, CIE, OBE, IDSM, who commanded the unit for eleven years.

During the early part of the visit to India from November 1921 to March 1922 of His Royal Highness the Prince of the Wales, Maharaja of Patiala sent him a formal invitation to visit Patiala as a state guest. The invitation was graciously accepted and the Prince stayed at Patiala for three memorable days from 22 to 24 February 1922. Based on the dispatches forwarded by the special correspondent of the *Pioneer* London, who had accompanied the Royal guest, a few pertinent excerpts datelined Patiala which appeared in the paper in London on 22 February 1922 are reproduced:- "When the Prince arrived at Patiala this morning it was, of course, his first introduction to the martial Punjab. The drive to the Motibagh Palace via the Mall Road with His Highness the Maharaja, who had been the first to greet him at the station, was through thousands of warlike Sikhs, who cheered vociferously and gave the Prince a great reception. Almost immediately after the public arrival there was a review of the State troops on the polo ground, four battalions of infantry, two regiments of cavalry and some artillery being on parade. Patiala is famed for its army, and one was struck by the smartness of the men in their general evolutions and, in fact, the serviceable character of the whole parade. The troops were led past His Royal Highness by the Maharaja in person, who is also the Commander-in-Chief of his forces. The gallop past of the artillery and cavalry towards the end of the parade was most thrilling and very cleverly executed. It was a gallop of the unvarnished order, where spur and knee played their all importants part. Before the march past His Royal Highness inspected the troops, and enroute to the end of the long line had to pass a great mass of pensioners who have come in from the surrounding districts. In this review parade the 1st Patiala Rajindra Sikh was adjudged to be the best contingent amongst the four infantry battalions of Patiala State".

Between 1923-24 regular yearly training was conducted in the Shiwalik Hills by the battalion, as part of the Ambala Brigade. The lessons learnt during World War I were applied to rigorous training. Furthermore, as the Patiala Army attached considerable importance to sports, various sports competitions were held on Inter-State level at Ambala. The Patiala forces invariably came on top. This tradition was in consonance with the love for sports with the Patiala State rulers.

In 1934 Colonel Balwant Singh Sidhu, CBE, OBI, DSO assumed the command of the battalion and remained its Commanding Officer for a decade.

7

The Patialas in World War II

From the middle of 1939, with the provocative and expansionist designs of Nazi Germany under Hitler having thrown all caution to the winds, war in Europe was more than imminent. Hitler's blitzkrieg through Poland was the last straw. War was declared on September 3, 1939. Thereafter the axis powers under Nazi Germany made rapid strides in overrunning numerous other European states before focusing attention against Stalin's forces in Russia. With fighting between the axis and allied powers also hinging around Asia Minor, it was then felt that Germany would also advance towards India from the northwest after overrunning Egypt, Syria, Iraq and Persia. As a result a number of Indian regular and state force units were moved to north-west India with a view to improve the defences on that approach.

When the Japanese attacked Pearl Harbour on 7 December 1941, substantial troops of Indian army, to include 1st Patiala Infantry, were also drawn into the war.

It was not until Germany's rapid advance into Russia had been checked at Stalingrad that the allies, particularly the British government in India, realized that a new threat was developing on the eastern frontier of India as a result of a rapid Japanese advance through south east Asia. This called for raising more troops to face this new challenge.

1st Patiala Rajindra Sikh Infantry was mobilized in October 1939 and carried out intensive training till the end of the year. By early 1940 the War Establishment of all States Forces was brought at par with regular army units, and the battalion was once again re-organised on the higher scale of manpower and brought to the strength of 814 all ranks.

Under the command of Colonel Balwant Singh Sidhu, the Rajindra Sikhs left Patiala on 16 June 1940 for Waziristan in North-West Frontier Province (NWFP). Reaching there four days later, it formed part of the Razmak Brigade. During its ten months tenure there, it operated in North Waziristan, where it took part in the offensive operations conducted against the adversaries based at Tappi and Tauda China village fortifications, where its performance was of an extremely high order indeed.

During November 1940 the unit was affiliated to the First Infantry Brigade (Abbottabad) and remained with it throughout the war. In April 1941 the unit moved to Abbottabad. From there it joined the forces of the common ally Ahmed Khel, and soon took part in the famous Tochi Valley operations, under very severe conditions, again in NWFP. In October 1941 the unit had the unique distinction of doing away with Special Service Officers, much to its relief!

In early April 1942 the unit, as part of First Infantry Brigade, was sent hurriedly to the Indo-Burma frontier to reinforce the front and to stem the tide of Japanese advance into India. It covered the withdrawal of the Burma Army in May 1942, and held the front for many months. The true worth of the unit soon became apparent when, under most unfavourable conditions of weather and terrain, and in a totally new environment, it soon established ascendancy over the Japanese. This by itself was a great achievement.

1st Patiala patrols, which had marched deep into Burma, found that the Japanese did not pursue the Burma Army beyond the line of the Chindwin River. Thus there was a large 'no-man's land' which the unit dominated to facilitate the Burma Army to be refitted and regrouped. The unit continued to play a stellar role through the rainy season of 1942.

Some prominent examples of endurance, which the Patialas had set, are mentioned in some of the letters held with the battalion. One of them, written by GOC 4 Corps (letter No. 234-G dated 7 November 1942), and addressed to the Commanding Officer, reads:

"I wish to draw attention to the good work which has been performed by the First Patiala Infantry. For about three months the battalion has occupied the forward positions of their Brigade front. They moved to these positions at the height of the monsoon period, when the most unfavourable and difficult climate conditions prevailed. These conditions caused great personal hardship to the troops and made communications very uncertain. The delivery of supplies to the forward posts was always a serious problem and, at times, rations had to be considerably reduced. In addition to manning the forward posts, the battalion sent out constant patrols to forward areas. These involved long marches, the crossing of rivers in spate and sleeping in the mosquito and leech infested jungles in adverse weather. One of the most striking achievements of these patrols was carried out by the Commanding Officer himself involving a force of 118 officers and men. 331 miles were covered by this special patrol in 21 days, including 88 miles through almost virgin jungle, at a time when weather conditions were at their worst. Considerable hardships were met and overcome with determination. Owing to the excellent condition of the men, only four fell sick."

The other letter was from 23 Division, addressed to the Commander, 1 Infantry Brigade. (letter no. G/59/0/78 (date illegible) of 1942). It says: "The Divisional Commander is very pleased with the work now being done by First Patiala. Will you very kindly convey his appreciation to Commanding Officer First Patiala and the officers and men of the battalion."

Based on a Reuters report, the prominent paper *The Statesman'* in its London edition dated 9 December 1942 stated under bold headlines: "Indian Patrol in the Wilds of Burma Crossed Flooded Rivers By Daring Method". It went on to state:

"A patrol consisting of officers and men of a famous Indian State Regiment, 1st Patiala, covered 360 miles in 16 marching days on a special mission into the Japanese occupied wilds of Burma, frequently crossed flooded rivers by means of daring improvisations. Boats of any kind would only have been dashed to pieces in the rapids. One method was to tie one end of a length of a rope or wire to a tree or a post and the other to a heavy log, which was then set a float near a bend of a river. The force of current carried the log across to the other side of the bend and held it there fairly firmly. Using the rope or wire as a handgrip, a man made his way across to

The Patialas in World War II

the log and fastened the other end to a firm support. The rest of the patrol then followed".

During the winter of 1942, the unit established a bridgehead across the Chindwin river to facilitate the crossing of the famous First Wingate Expedition, and later it advanced through four days march east of the river to take the weight off Wingate's men, thus ensuring their smooth withdrawal westwards. All this was done with the greatest zeal and enthusiasm, so typical of Patiala soldiers.

Having trained with British armoured corps units in the spring of 1943, 1st Patiala went down further into Burma with light tanks to probe Japanese presence, and soon contact was established at Kabaw Valley. The Japanese had also brought forward light tanks. 1st Patiala men, escorting allied tanks, gave a good account of themselves in this encounter, which took the enemy by total surprise. The latter suffered six casualties, and no loss came to Patiala forces.

Relevant extracts of a letter dated 13 June 1943, which originated from the GOC 23 Infantry Division, and was addressed to Colonel Balwant Singh Sidhu Bahadur, CBE, DSO, OBI, Commanding Officer First Patiala Infantry, states:

> "I would like on my departure to send a special message to First Patiala who, under your very able leadership, have done so well. Their discipline, turnout, soldierly bearing and physique have been a model. Their capacity to march long distances with heavy loads and to endure hardship has been unsurpassed by any other troops in this division.
>
> Their patrolling has been carried out with determination and with that guile which is necessary in dealing with an enemy like the Japanese. You have met the enemy face to face and have inflicted

on him casualties greater than those, which you yourself suffered, and you have, in short, established over him a moral superiority which is so essential in winning battles.

There is no doubt that the early patrolling carried out by your regiment on the eastern bank of the Chindwin had a great effect, and your subsequent movement eastwards to Kaungkashi produced the required result by taking the weight off the returning parties of 'Longcloth' (referring to Major General Orde Wingate). Last summer your patrol activities in the Kabaw Valley contributed towards the re-establishment of our influence over that area. I am sure that when later on you are called upon to take part in the general offensive against the Japanese, you will do so with that stubborn ferocity so characteristic of the Sikh Soldier.

Good Wishes and Good Luck to You All. Wahe Guru Ji Ka Khalsa, Sri Wahe Guru Ji Ki Fateh."

In early 1944, when the Japanese launched their famous March to Delhi, the unit was constantly engaged in operations to cut the enemy's line of communication or to turn its flanks. Again, in the spring of 1944, it went probing deeper into Burma, but the Japanese had a design to make a bid to reach the Indian plains in Assam via Kohima. On learning this, 1st Patiala and other troops hurriedly got back to the hills overlooking Imphal plains. When the Japanese cut Kohima-Imphal road, the troops covering the Imphal plains alongwith all civilians living there entrenched themselves to form fortified defensive positions. It was at this time that the Commanding Officer of 1st Patiala volunteered to cut the Japanese route via Ukhrul to Kohima, and he was permitted to do so. He took the battalion

The Patialas in World War II

through a jungle route and contacted the retreating Japanese troops at Sakpao, on the Imphal-Ukhrul track, after the Japanese bid on Kohima failed. 1st Patiala engaged a retreating and demoralized enemy unit, causing heavy losses to it.

During May and June 1944 the unit resorted to some of the fiercest fighting under the worst possible weather conditions and in rough, treacherous country. In all its engagements the battalion never lost any position it intended to hold, and took every position it attacked. It had the satisfaction of contributing a vital share in throwing the Japanese back across the frontier of India into Burma in August 1944.

The *'Indian Information'*, an official weekly of the army, in its issue dated 15 September 1944, described a particular battle as follows:

> "A battalion of the First Patiala Infantry has gained many successes against the Japanese on the Imphal front. One of their most recent objectives was a hill feature east of Imphal – a good observation post, nearly 4,600 feet high and 15 miles across from where they were. The enemy was well dug - in on its steep height and isolated from all directions. One morning Naik Mohinder Singh, having served for 11 years in the battalion and an experienced soldier, went with another Naik and silently crept into the enemy position. After staying there for four hours, gauging enemy defences, he returned to his headquarters and volunteered to take a section into the midst of the enemy position. Permission was granted.
>
> The same evening one of the Patiala companies took off, arriving behind the enemy lines of communication next morning at an appointed time. Later another

company was sent to approach the enemy position from the north, but it remained in hiding until the signal was given to attack. When the 'okay' signal was received from both the companies, Naik Mohinder Singh and his section slowly crept towards the enemy position and lay in wait there. Half an hour later the company, coming from the north, launched a vigorous attack and the enemy opened fire. Immediately Naik Mohinder and his section shouted 'Sat Sri Akal' from the centre of the enemy position itself, which was followed by the attacking company simultaneously yelling the same war cry. The enemy was utterly confused, stopped firing and dispersed immediately, leaving the feature to the Patialas who occupied the position without suffering any casualties. While one retreating Japanese was killed, many others were wounded. The enemy, however, did not retreat along its established lines of communication in order to avoid suffering a worse fate; instead, it scattered indiscriminately".

During the later part of the rainy season of 1944, the whole Burma Corps advanced through most inclement weather and pushed the Japanese finally out of India, opening the way to re-occupy Burma. Field Marshal Slim had this to say about the Patialas:

"I want it conveyed to 1st Patiala that if I were to pick one unit for any special task, it would be 1st Patiala. I am sanctioning a special one month's leave to the whole unit at Shillong".

However, while spending only a portion of its earned leave at Shillong, enjoying its salubrious climates, 1st Patiala received orders to move to Bombay for combined inter service operations. This meant a switch overland of over

The Patialas in World War II

3000 km. Nevertheless, the unit took it at its stride, reaching there by November 1944. Unfamiliar with sea operations, but through rigorous training, the unit got fully accustomed to a variety of naval boats, combat and landing crafts within a few months, and was soon fully acquainted with the nuances of sea-borne attack. This unique quality of adaptability was to become a hallmark of the unit.

In order to facilitate other units to carry out training, and due to lack of space for a large number of troops in Bombay, the unit was ordered to concentrate at Nasik, where it soon established camp and carried out its own training. It was here that Colonel Balwant Singh Sidhu (who later became a Lieutenant General) relinquished command of the unit by the end of 1944 and Lieutenant Colonel Bikramdev Singh Gill, DSO, took over the reins of the battalion.

On 9 August 1945, when news broke out that the mighty Japanese army had surrendered following the dropping of atom bombs by the US Air Force at Hiroshima and Nagasaki in Japan, it became difficult to believe that a formidable enemy like Japan would surrender en masse. However, in spite of the surrender, Headquarters of South East Asia Command (SEAC), under the command of British Admiral Lord Louis Mountbatten, took the decision to carry out the amphibious landings at Malaya, as planned. By July 1945 the unit was declared fully fit and battle worthy for amphibious operations.

The 1st Patialas, with a strength of 809 all ranks, left Nasik for Bombay on 30 August 1945. The troops embarked on a Landing Craft Infantry – Large (LCI – L) named 'Arawa' at Alexandria Docks, Colaba, Bombay, by the same evening. This ship formed part of a convoy of eleven ships consisting of Landing Ship Tanks (LST), Landing Craft Utility (LCU),

LCI-L, logistics and Naval escort ships. The flotilla sailed out of Bombay on 2 September. As the voyage was a considerably long one, a large number of officers and men became seasick on board for many days. The sea was rough most of the days, and the 'Arawa' was a small vessel comparatively. As a result it was more prone to rolling and pitching, thus increasing chances of seasickness for the uninitiated. In spite of these problems it was a very interesting and thrilling experience for the Patialas, as none had ever sailed before !

The ship sailed southwards until it crossed the southern tip of Ceylon, where the headquarters of SEAC was located, and then sailed eastwards crossing the 10 Degree Channel between the Andman and Nicobar group of Islands, which was held by the Japanese army. The Patialas crossed the channel silently in the hours of darkness. Thereafter the flotilla headed towards the Strait of Malacca and entered its placid waters between Malaya and the island of Jawa, then a part of Netherland East Indies.

On the morning of 12 September the unit once again saw land, and the same afternoon it disembarked at Port Diskson, on the western coast of Malaya. In the evening it left the Port to capture Seramban, the capital of Negri Sembilan, the centre of a vast rubber producing district. After a night march of 24 miles the unit entered Seramban in the early hours of the 13th and occupied its allotted sector after brushing aside minor opposition. During the next few days a big victory march was carried out through the main streets of the town. Lieutenant General Roberts, Corps Commander of 34 Corps and the General Officer Commanding Malaya theatre took the salute. Troops from all the three services took part, and more than 39,000 locals turned out to watch the spectacular show. The Patialas, too, did very well during the march past. Next morning both the Divisional and Brigade Commanders came forward to congratulate the Commanding Officer and to personally convey their appreciation for the very smart turnout, exemplary bearing and first class march past of the battalion during the victory march. They also mentioned that the contingent put up by the Rajindra Sikhs was adjudged the best, and the battalion prominently stood out amongst all the units which took part in the grand victory march.

On 20 September all available troops of 1st Patiala established various guards and pickets throughout the town of nearby Sagamet, where a similar victory parade was held. Owing to unavoidable absence of the Brigade Commander of 1st Infantry Brigade, Colonel Bikramdev Singh Gill, DSO, Commanding Officer 1st Patiala took the salute. In the morning, before the parade, the unit held a 'bhog' ceremony of an Akhand Path, as per its rich traditions.

The Patialas arrived at Port Dickson on the 25th, and six hundred all ranks embarked once again, on much smaller landing crafts, for Java on 28 September. This time the men, having already had the experience of sailing in high seas, remained well and happy, unlike the sea-sickness felt by many during their trip from India to Malaya. The latest voyage was most enjoyable and the unit landed on 3 October at Batavia, now known as Jakarta in Java, which is a large Island of the Dutch East Indies. It was also under Japanese occupation till their surrender. Java, Sumatra, Borneo and various other islands now form Indonesia. The unit was responsible for maintaining law and order in the central sector of the vast and beautiful city of Batavia where all was not very peaceful, and the unit had to shoot at enemy troops and guerillas every now and then.

Owing to shipping difficulties, the unit had to leave four officers and 200 men in Malaya, but they rejoined soon enough. That apart, another 250 men alongwith some mules were also left behind at Nasik. As a result, the battalion was dispersed in three different and far flung countries !

A number of operations were also carried out against local guerrillas, mostly freedom fighters fighting for independence, and armed bandits. The objective was to re-establish the Dutch regime, since their own troops were too enfeebled due to long captivity, and proved to be no match to the motivated local rebels who were armed and trained by the Japanese. The Indonesian guerillas were up in arms against the Dutch and wanted independence. 1st Patiala plunged into a war like situation against the invisible but aggressive young Indonesian guerrillas, and acquitted themselves most creditably. The Patiala men also spent some time at Buithnzorg, Bandung and Tjindtore, amongst others towns. In all these places the unit had to resort to stiff fighting against well trained, highly motivated and well armed bandits.

During its tenure in Java the battalion performed all assigned tasks in a commendable manner. Although a number of examples of heroism and valour are available with the unit, I would like to mention a particular episode —an example of raw guts, grit and presence of mind.

During mid April 1946, 1st Patiala was escorting a large number of Dutch personnel and their families from the Indonesian capital Jakarta to the city of Bandung, some 150 miles to the southeast; through an area infested with armed Indonesian freedom fighters. As its unwieldy convoy approached a night camp at Soeka Bumi, there was a long cutting on the road some two miles from the town. The

Indonesians hurled grenades and fired automatics from an unassailable height. In the failing light the Patialas' response was not very effective, and they suffered some casualties. However, they forced their way into the camp, which was a small post of surrendered Japanese soldiers, and the latter were very helpful to the Patialas in warding off the guerrillas.

Next morning, as the leading escort vehicle was getting into position, an Indonesian boy, hardly 13-14 years old, lobbed a grenade into the vehicle which was jampacked with troops, thus throwing them into near panic and utter disorder as there was no room for manoeuvre. However, undeterred, a 19 years old sepoy named Bakshish Singh picked up the grenade and threw it back at the Indonesian boy, killing him instantaneously. This young sepoy showed extreme courage at great personal risk, thereby saving many comrades from certain death or serious injury. Bakshish Singh became a watchword in the unit. The Commanding Officer, Lieutenant Colonel Bikramdev Singh, DSO, recommended the sepoy for a George Cross. However, he was awarded a Mentioned-in-Despatches. The awards are a fortune of war, no doubt, but the unit was shocked indeed. Nevertheless, the sepoy remains an unsung hero till date. Here one is reminded of the famous lines of Shakespeare pertaining to timely initiative –

"There is a tide in the affairs of men,
Which, taken at the flood, leads to fortunes;
Omitted, all the voyage of their life
Is bound in shallows and miseries"

While at Java the unit handled the unpleasant and complicated situation very tactfully, which earned the appreciation of the General Officer Commanding Allied Force in Netherland East Indies; the Dutch and the

Indonesian civil authorities and also the freedom fighters fighting for independence.

The battalion left Batavia during the end of June 1946 and landed at Calcutta on 8 July 1946, after having been on active service for over six years. It reached Patiala on 12 July 1946 and was given a grand reception by His Highness and the State citizens. Brigadier N.D. Wingrove, commanding the First (Abbottabad) Indian Infantry Brigade, appreciated the service of the unit through a letter which stated:

> "On the eve of your departure from Java, I wish to place on record the appreciation and gratitude of all ranks of the First (Abbottabad) Indian Infantry Brigade, for magnificent work your battalion has done for the Brigade during the long period you have been associated with it. Your record of war service is outstanding and second to none. You have fought side by side with British, Indian and Gurkha troops, and have proved worthy of your place amongst the greatest fighters of the world. Your battalion can be justly proud of its magnificent achievements in the cause of Peace and Freedom. In Java your work has been of the highest order in which you have enhanced your already fine reputation.
>
> At all times the bearing and conduct of your men has been exemplary, and throughout these most difficult times, the discipline and smartness of all ranks of your battalion has been maintained at the highest level of peace time standards. Of the bravery and restlessness of your man in carrying out every task assigned to them, there is no doubt. After such a long space of active operations you have earned your forthcoming period of leave.

The Patialas in World War II

Your going will be a grievous loss to the Division and the Brigade; a replacement to equal you will be hard to find. You leave behind a tradition of loyalty and comradeship which will be an example to us all. Whilst we say goodbye with regret, we are pleased to know that your men have, at least, got their well earned rest. On behalf of us all I thank you for all that your battalion has done to make and maintain the high standard of our Brigade. You deserve well of your State, your country and our King Emperor. God speed and good luck".

From its six years of fighting in the dry hills of the NWFP against the wily Pathans, to the dense rain jungles of Burma and to fighting Indonesian guerrillas successfully, the Patialas gained a very rich and the best operational experience in an international military environment.

During World War II the Patialas earned a total of 83 awards to include one Commander British Empire (CBE), which had no parallel in the entire British Indian Army; two Distinguished Service Orders (DSO) awarded to both the Commanding Officers; one Member British Empire (MBE); nine Military Crosses (MCs); one Indian Order of Merit (IOM-II) Class – II; 12 Indian Distinguished Service Medals (IDSM); five Military Medals (MM), one British Empire Medal (BEM) and 51 Mentioned-in-Despatches.

DURING WORLD WAR II
NWFP

Brigadier Denys (extreme right), Colonel Freeland (second from right) and Colonel Balwant Singh Sidhu (extreme left) at Razmak- 1939

1st Patiala officers in front of their living quarters at Kakul-1941

1st Patiala at Gardil Camp (North Waziristhan) - January 1941

His Highness Maharaja Yadvinder Singh inspecting 1st Patiala troops at Patiala during War Leave-1944

The Maharaja of Patiala reviewing the impressive march past of 1st Patiala (Rajindra Sikhs) - 1945

AT PATIALA

1st Patiala on return from active service in NWFP - 1945

Presentation of colours to 1st Patiala at Patiala - 1945

IN SOUTH EAST ASIA

His Highness Yadvinder Singh, Maharaja of Patiala, reviewing 1st Patiala troops at Nasik, prior to leaving for Malaya -1945

Major Jaswant Singh (centre), 2IC 1st Patiala and officers bidding farewell to Charlie Company en route to Java at Port Dickson, Malaya-1945

Charlie Company of 1st Patiala disembarking at the port of Tondjonk Priok in Java-1945

Field Marshal Slim and Lieutenant General Christison conveying their gratitude to troops of 1st Patiala for their excellent performance in Batavia-Java-1945

His Highness being shown captured Japanese flag by Colonel Balwant Singh Sidhu, DSO

Battalion parading captured Japanese flags at Patiala Central Police Station ground-August 1946

Battalion returns to Patiala on 12 July 1946, after 7 years of active service

Sri Guru Granth Sahib of 1st Patiala passing through a street of Patiala on an ornamented elephant

8

Operations in Jammu & Kashmir (1947-48)

Trouble Brewing in Kashmir

Following India's Independence, the nation was passing through a traumatic experience of mass movement of lakhs of displaced men, women and children across the border. Simultaneously, a new situation was developing in Jammu and Kashmir (J&K) state which was to involve and put to test the fledgling Indian army which was still recognizing itself as a result of partition.

Like the state of Hyderabad, Maharaja Sri Hari Singh of J&K also did not opt for immediate integration and enjoyed an independent status through a Standstill Agreement valid for one year with effect from 15 August 1947. Pakistan took full advantage of this situation and planned an invasion of the state with meticulous care with a view to annex the state. The plan, code named 'Operation Gulmarg', was based on considerable strategic and tactical insight. It envisaged to split up the state's army into small groups and cause attrition to the splintered army through hit-and-run attacks all along the frontier with Pakistan.

Operations in Jammu & Kashmir (1947-48)

As per the plan conceived at Pakistan Army Headquarters, thousands of tribals and mercenaries, everready to take up arms for plunder and loot, were gathered at Peshawar and Rawalpindi. Every Pathan tribe was also required to enlist at least one 'Lashkar' of 1000 tribesmen. After enlistment, these mercenaries and Lashkars were to be concentrated at Bannu, Wana, Peshawar, Kohat, Thal and Naushera by the first week of September 1947. According to the plan, the local formation commanders at these places were to issue them arms, ammunition and some essential items of clothing issued against some Pakistan regular army units. Each tribal Lashkar was also to be provided with a Major, a Captain and ten JCOs of the regular Pakistan army who, on paper, were shown to be on official leave.

Plan and Conditions for Invasion

For the conduct of operations in the valley, the broad outline of the operational plan was in three parts. The first was for six Lashkars to advance along the main road from Muzaffarabad to Srinagar via Domel, Uri and Baramula, with the specific task of capturing the aerodrome and subsequently advancing to the Banihal Pass. The next part involved two Lashkars to advance from the Haji Pir Pass direct on to Gulmarg, thereby securing the right flank of the main force advancing from Muzaffarabad. The third part involved a similar force of two Lashkars to advance from Tithwal, through the Nastachun Pass, for the capture of Sopore, Handwara and Bandipur. In the Jammu sector another force of 10 Lashkars was to operate in the Punch, Bhimbar and Rawla areas with the intention of capturing Punch and Rajauri and then advancing to Jammu.

The 'D' day for 'Operation Gulmarg' was fixed as 22 October 1947, on which date the various Lashkars were to cross into Jammu and Kashmir territory. It was envisaged to make optimal use of the rugged terrain and the demographic imbalance existing in the state.

The Pakistani focus was on three distinct regions, namely the Jammu region in the south, the Kashmir region further north and the Ladakh region towards the east. Each region is divided by lofty mountain ranges. Whereas the height of the ranges around Jammu region varies from 500 to 2000 metres, around the Kashmir region it extends up to more than 4000 metres. Ladakh is completely a high altitude region where the air is rarefied and the surroundings are above 5000 metres. Demographically, in the Jammu region the population is mainly Hindu, except for the areas of Punch and the northern reaches of Rajouri and Doda, which comprise a majority of Muslim population. Further up north, the Kashmir region also comprises a Muslim majority population, while Ladakh is basically a Buddhist region, except for Kargil which comprises a Shia Muslim majority population.

With everything in Pakistan's favour, the operations were launched with the fury of an avalanche. But for their initial mistakes and lack of drive in leadership at the lower level, the history of J & K State would have taken an entirely different turn.

The J&K State Forces, like other state forces in the pre-independence era, were organized under the overall control of a British officer. Major General H.L. Scott was the Chief of Staff of J&K State Forces. The state army was organized into four infantry brigade headquarters located at Srinagar, Jammu, Punch and Jhangar respectively. Besides other supporting arms and services there were a total of nine J&K Rifle battalions and small garrison units distributed under various brigades. All these forces were spread out all along the border and in the interior, at times

Operations in Jammu & Kashmir (1947-48)

in company, platoon and section strength. Unaware of the coming invasion, the state force troops were already committed in tiny groups. They were not geared up to repel any aggression but to carry out normal garrison duties. Apart from that, confusion caused as a result of mass migration of the population from across the border, large scale killings and free movement of thousands of armed gangs, more for self-protection than mischief, proved to be ideal conditions for the invaders.

'Operation Gulmarg' Launched

The main column in the north advanced on Murree-Domel-Srinagar road on 22 October with the explicit aim of capturing Srinagar, the nearby airfield and blocking the Valley at Banihal. It consisted of 5,000 men, all well-armed and equipped with rifles, LMGs, MMGs and mortars. Their transport consisted of about 300 civilian lorries, adequately provisioned for petrol and supplies.

There was hardly any opposition to this large force. A weak battalion of the State Army – the 4th Jammu and Kashmir Rifles, was spread out over a large area in small sub-units. The frontier outpost fell on 22 October itself followed by Domel the next day. Two Muslim companies of the battalion in Muzaffarabad, after killing the commanding officer and a large number of their erstwhile Dogra comrades, deserted and joined the invaders with all their unit arms and ammunition. From then on it was a virtual walk-over for the Pakistanis at Garhi, Chenari and Chakothi.

Brigadier Rajinder Singh, who had since taken over as Chief of Staff from Major General Scott, personally went forward to direct the operations. Before the invaders reached Uri he had the steel girder bridge of Uri destroyed to gain time, as a result of which he gained four days of respite to organize basic defences with just about 200 men then under him. Fleeing Hindu and Sikh refugees further complicated matters for his hard pressed force.

As the enemy forces advanced towards Srinagar on 24 October, the few gallant men under Brigadier Rajinder Singh tried hard to delay them. In this futile bid the Brigadier was killed and his men withdrew towards the heights east of Baramula. Soon the enemy reached Mahura, where the thermal power plant, the main source of electricity to the state capital, was damaged. As a result Srinagar was plunged into darkness and much panic prevailed in the city.

Baramula, some 55 kilometres to the west of the capital, was then plundered. It was free for all, and this went on for three days. With all command and control virtually lost, hundreds of the marauders went back to their homes in the accompanying civilian lorries with their booty. Their advance to Srinagar was therefore naturally held up. Srinagar, which was within their grasp only for the asking, thus slipped out of their hands forever.

Indian Intervention

Seeing the hopeless situation, Maharaja Sri Hari Singh signed the Instrument of Accession and acceded to India on 26 October, following which immediate action was then taken by India to send troops to help the state repel aggression.1 Sikh, then based at Gurgaon area for the conduct of internal security duties, was immediately collected together and the first aircraft carrying its troops landed at the Srinagar airfield the next day by 9.30 am on 27 October 1947.

By the last day of October the strength of Indian troops in the Valley comprised Headquarters 161 Infantry Brigade,

Operations in Jammu & Kashmir (1947-48)

1 Sikh, 1 Para, elements of 4 Kumaon and 1 Mahar (MG). The Jammu region comprised 3 Para and one company of 1 Mahar (MG). Thereafter, with 1 Para, 3 Para and two companies of 4 Kumaon under Major Somnath Sharma having reached the Valley, 161 Infantry Brigade under Brigadier J.C. Katoch was formed. As a result the enemy was held at a distance of about 6-8 kilometres from the state capital, and the defence of the airfield was also ensured. However, in the process Brigadier Katoch was wounded in the leg by a chance bullet and had to be evacuated. His place was taken over by Colonel Harbaksh Singh on 2 November, and shortly afterwards Brigadier L.P. Sen arrived and assumed command. On 5 November Major General Kalwant Singh also reached Srinagar by air and assumed command of the newly created J&K Division headquartered in Srinagar.

The Patialas in Jammu & Kashmir

The unit had hardly settled down in Patiala after World War – II when it was called to deal with the partition and post-independence disturbances. While it was deployed in this task, it received the clarion call to move into the state of Jammu & Kashmir for meeting the new challenge being faced by the state from the Pakistani sponsored marauders. It was flown to Jammu on 3 November 1947 under the command of Lieutenant Colonel Bikramdev Singh Gill, DSO.

Immediately on arrival at Jammu, the unit was employed in active patrolling and internal security duties with the objectives of tracking enemy movements, pin-pointing location of enemy and own troops on the Indian side of the border; and also to restore confidence amongst the local population around Kahne Chak and Dewa Batala in the Chhamb Sector.

In spite of these intensive tasks being performed by the unit, two of its companies moved on orders to Banihal, Ramban and Kud areas where the Patialas conducted small scale operations successfully. From 17 November 1947, the unit was placed under command 268 Infantry Brigade and till the end of November it was employed on tasks related to securing the vital lines of communication of 50 Para Brigade. The unit carried out this task by intensive patrolling from firm bases at Naushera, Beripattan, Chauki-Chaura, Tanda and Akhnoor. The Unit had to do all this task without two companies which were operating in Banihal and Ramban areas.

On 24 November 1947, the battalion was ordered to secure a bridgehead in Beripattan near Sunderbani to facilitate the advance of elements of 50 Parachute Brigade. One company less one platoon was also ordered to contact the Beripattan garrison, which had been cut off. The company had its first skirmish with the enemy three miles short of Beripattan, and succeeded in recovering some wounded and stragglers of the outpost who had lost all hopes of survival. The task was successfully carried out and the enemy suffered heavy casualties. The company brought back valuable information for further operations in that area.

By the end of November 1947, two brigade headquarters and two additional infantry battalions had crossed the Ravi river over a pontoon bridge with some elements of light transport. At that time 1st Patiala was not brigaded and was theatre reserve. The unit was being rushed to other threatened flashpoints, mostly areas of Naushera and Jhangar.

On 4 December 1947, the battalion less two companies, with a troop of armoured cars of 7 Cavalry under command and a battery of field guns in support, left Akhnoor for operations in the western parts which were in a most disturbed condition. The highlight of this operation was the personal orders given by JAK Force Commander, who also saw off the Patiala troops moving out. By this time the Pakistani raiders were very close to Akhnoor, indulging in plunder, loot, arson and threatening to blow up the bridge over the Chenab. The unit column less two companies reached Palanwala, having swept the area bounded by low hills in the north and the Chenab in the south. During this sweep the unit had several small skirmishes with isolated enemy troops and captured or killed a number of raiders. A troop of 7 Cavalry also operated with the battalion in these operations. Orders were then being finalised by higher headquarters for the capture of Chhamb.

Battle of Chhamb

By early December 1947 it was reported that Pakistani marauders armed with automatic weapons and 2" mortars were threatening to isolate Jammu from Naushera, Rajouri and Punch by planning to seize the only bridge over the Chenab at Akhnoor. Several thousand raiders who had started from Gujarat district of Pakistan crossed the state boundary at Bhimber and reached Chhamb practically unopposed and established themselves at the Manawar Ki Tawi, a fast flowing river.

In the first week of December 1948, the threat to Akhnoor bridge seemed imminent. Thousands of Indian refugees from Chhamb-Jaurian-Palanwala areas began to trek back towards Jammu carrying whatever meager belongings they could on their heads, and in the process the Akhnoor bridge was virtually choked. At this stage, on 7 December, 1st Patiala was ordered to recapture Chhamb which had fallen into Pak hands, and hold the banks of the Manawar Ki Tawi at all cost.

Enemy dispositions were reported from Mandiala to Munawar along the western bank of Munawar Tawi river, as the enemy appreciated that this area was most ideally suited for Indian troops to cross over and head for the Deva-Batala-Bhimber area. The ground forward (west) of Palanwala was open and the approach to the road-river crossing was dominated by observation and fire from the Chhamb position, where just 10 days back a Madras company alongwith a troop of armoured cars grouped with a section of MMGs had suffered major casualties and had to abandon the crossing. The enemy thereafter had gained ten days to improve its defensive positions, as it was convinced that Indian troops would definitely attempt a crossing in this area.

The battalion alongwith three companies, supported by a troop of field guns, a platoon of mortars, section MMGs and two armoured cars concentrated at Palanwala for further operation. The plan was to cross the river northwest of Chapreal, three miles upstream from Chhamb crossing and flank around point 892 with two companies, with a platoon of mortars and a section of MMGs supporting from the eastern bank. 'A' company was to act as a right flank guard in Samuan Chapreal area. Two platoons, armoured car troops and a section of MMG were to execute a straight crossing on a wide front. The river was 2 feet deep and 80 yards wide and current speed 4 miles per hour. Having crossed, 'C' and 'D' companies moved southwards towards the right and left respectively and established on high ground northwest of Mandiala.

On 8 December the Patialas reached the northern bank of the Manawar Tawi and opened fire with LMGs and 3" mortars, giving the impression to Pak raiders that a frontal attack was imminent. Two rifle companies crossed the Tawi four kilometres upstream and descended on the surprised

Operations in Jammu & Kashmir (1947-48)

raiders who had concentrated in an orchard belonging to an honorary Indian Captain. 35 Pak bodies, complete with rifles and equipment, were captured by sunset. By that time two supporting 3.7" Howitzers alongwith a detachment of field ambulance got into the Patiala camp, and there was hardly any time to dig in. Brigadier (later Lieutenant General) Lakhinder Singh, the local formation commander, also joined the Patiala by late evening.

By nightfall the raiders set up bonfires all around the Patiala camp. They were sure that they would eventually overwhelm Patiala troops. Some four to five thousand raiders then got into Chhamb village and, with the beating of drums, they started firing intensely. The CO, Lieutenant Colonel (later Brigadier) Bikram Dev Singh, DSO, issued quick but simple orders - "Fight till the last man". Only thirty yards separated the defenders from the raiders, who were firing from behind a wall. The Indian 3.7" Howitzers fired with open sights like rifles. Their flash was blinding and report deafening. Legend has it that the fire from two sides of the Patiala camp looked like Diwali fireworks. The CO was calm and collected, sipping his special brand of drink. All along 1st Patiala Sikh troops stood like rock, equally unruffled. Whenever the unnerved Brigadier Lakhinder mumbled something, the CO said "Relax, do not worry, sir, have a drink", and a fully charged glass was immediately handed over, only to be swallowed down in a gulp by the Brigadier.

'A' company was now doing left flank guard. The battalion headquarters, MMG's and Mortars now moved parallel to forward troops on the eastern bank and supported their advance. 'A' company, having moved south, began combing the area in front of battalion headquarters, and encountered 12 fanatical Pathans infiltrating into the company area taking advantage of the tall *sarkanda* and engaged them heavily. Lance Havildar Jawala Singh, in command of No 2 platoon, lead his party under a great personal risk in such a way as to surround the Pathans. He killed five and the remaining got lost in the tall *sarkanda* and probably became casualties.

As they moved down to Mandiala both 'C' and 'D' companies were heavily engaged by the enemy from a copse around the village. Both the companies, using clever fire and movement drills, cleared the village killing or wounding at least 20 enemy soldiers. Two snipers gave a particularly difficult time to the left forward platoon of 'D' company. Lance Naik Phuman Singh, regardless of intense enemy fire, stalked to a grenade throwing distance and hurled a grenade, thereby killing both the snipers. His heroic act earned him a Vir Chakra. His citation stated that – "On 10 December 1947, during the attack on Mandiala in Jammu & Kashmir, Lance Havildar Phuman Singh was in command of a section of the left forward platoon which was held up by accurate fire from two enemy snipers, from well protected and concealed positions. Lance Naik Phuman Singh, utterly regardless of the intense fire, stalked alone to within grenade throwing distance and killed both the snipers, thus clearing the way for his platoon for further advance. Another sniper shot at him from 10 yards. He escaped narrowly, but this only infuriated him. With amazing speed he put his bayonet through the sniper. In these two actions he displayed remarkable grit and set a fine example of selfless devotion to duty, individual gallantry and high skill at arms."

In another incident that day Havildar Seva Singh also earned a Vir Chakra. His citation reads: "On 10 December 1947, Havildar Seva Singh was in command of a forward platoon during flanking movement to the east of Chhamb. His own platoon was being heavily sniped at. He went to the foremost man of his platoon and carried out useful reconnaissance from a completely exposed position, showing utter disregard for his personal safety. Having located an enemy resistance point, without waiting for orders, he made up his mind to take the platoon by a dash. He personally led the platoon, charged into the forward enemy line and encouraged his men to blitz through. The men responded splendidly to his inspiring call and the enemy position was charged by bayonets after a fierce hand-to-hand battle. Havildar Seva Singh displayed an outstanding will to win. His cheerful and inspiring leadership and gallant action set a fine example."

The battalion headquarters party were at this stage engaged by another sniper who, from a very close and concealed position, held them up for half an hour. Sepoy Ram Singh of 'A' company, whose section was nearby, spotted the sniper and killed him thus enabling the battalion headquarters to resume advance instantaneously.

Soon 'C' and 'D' companies arrived barely 200 yards northeast of Chhamb, and both the companies were heavily engaged by enemy MMGs and LMGs fired from the centre of Chhamb village, and further advance was stalled. At this stage the guns and unit mortars could not support the companies due to the close proximity of the enemy. Here both the company commander's, that is Major Shamsher Singh and Captain Hazura Singh displayed outstanding leadership and courage fighting every inch of ground, bitterly contested by the enemy. 2' mortars and grenade dischargers gave a good account of themselves. At least 10 snipers were killed and many others forced out. 'C' company made a further detour to the west of the village to surround the defenders. The company, after stiff fighting, got to within 400 yards of Chhamb.

Soon both 'C' and 'D' companies were unable to make any further progress due to heavy fire coming from a plantation south west of the village. Both companies again engaged the enemy with 2' mortars, grenade dischargers and LMG's. The enemy, though literally surrounded, stubbornly resisted further advance of the Patialas and were firing frantically from their posts.

As a result of the most dauntless and determined will shown by the two forward companies, the impregnable position was captured by 3.30 p.m. Throughout the day, a high degree of cooperation was displayed by the affiliated troops, including those of the field guns. That apart, the timely support of the MMG platoon and armoured car greatly assisted the operation.

The firefight continued till late into the night, and gradually an eerie silence fell towards dawn. At first light the balance of Patiala troops searched the area. They saw blood-marked trails of a number of dragged dead bodies, and considerable equipment was left behind. By mid-day the troops reached a high ground near Chhamb overlooking the distant Amrala Headworks of Pakistan, with its numerous shimmering lights. The Patialas heaved a sigh of relief, and so did the higher formations operating in Jammu & Kashmir.

Following this battle innumerable congratulatory messages began pouring in from higher commanders on this incredible victory which put an end to the threat to the strategic Akhnoor bridge once and for all. The refugees soon returned home. The theatre commander, Lieutenant General Kulwant Singh, flew in to congratulate the unit.

On 12 December 1947, the unit was placed under command 80 Independent Brigade Group and was employed on intensive patrolling upto 18 December in border areas, north of Chhamb. In a defensive battle from 4.30 p.m. on 15 December till 3 a.m. on 16 December the unit broke up repeated enemy attacks which earned high appreciation from various commanders, including the Army Commander.

Operations in Jammu & Kashmir (1947-48)

From 20 December till the end of the month the Patialas were employed for various tasks related to the defence of the Akhnoor bridge over the Chenab; intensive patrolling and also protection of the lines of communication from Jammu to Noushera.

Naushera, Jammu and Samba

On 31 December 1947 the unit moved to Noushera where it formed part of 'Z' Brigade so as to relieve enemy pressure in that sector. Till 7 January 1948 the Patialas were employed in various local actions against the enemy who was trying to capture positions of tactical advantage for launching an attack on Noushera. It was also employed in road opening operations till it finally left Noushera on 15 January 1948 and reached Akhnoor a week later after having combed the whole area right upto Akhnoor. Thereafter the unit was employed for the defence of Jammu town with a subsidiary task of keeping the Jammu road open.

The unit soon came to be known as 'Mobile Patiala' and was always rushed from place to place wherever any threat occurred. One night Pakistani raiders entered Sambha area where only one unit was located, that is 2/3 Gorkha Rifles. The Patialas were asked to help the Gurkhas by sending a company. 'C' company under Major Shamsher Singh moved to Sambha over night on 25 January, did a flag march in the villages where raiders had been frequenting. As the border was close by, the raiders always crossed and recrossed the border during the night so as to loot Indian villages. The Patiala company was soon employed along the border and rejoined the unit after a week or so. It was again 'C' company which was sent to Samba area. During January and February the battalion must have made 11 to 12 trips between Jammu-Naushera for clearing the areas of raiders.

Due to enemy's attack on Naushera on 6 and 7 February 1948 the battalion was again rushed to help the hard pressed 50 Para Brigade. It was engaged in clearing positions around Naushera from 8 to 11 February 1948, and than reverted to Jammu on 13 February 1948 as a result of a sudden threat developing near Jammu. On 1 March the Patialas once again moved to Naushera where it was involved in some more offensive actions, such as the capture of Point 2916 on 2 March 1948 where the unit fought heroically earning two awards posthumously. While one was a Maha Vir Chakra (MVC), the other was a Vir Chakra (VrC).

The MVC was awarded to Subedar Gurdial Singh posthumously for the capture of Point 2916 and for his role in the battle of Jhangar, which is being described subsequently. His citation reads:

> "During an attack on a picquet in Jammu & Kashmir on 2 March 1948, Subedar Gurdial Singh was the leading platoon commander. An enemy mortar knocked out his leading section. Without being down-hearted or waiting for any order, he rushed down with his two sections. He threw a grenade at one bunker from 20 yards while the enemy was still firing ceaselessly, led a bayonet charge and was responsible for bayoneting two survivors. His courageous action filled the men with invincible spirit and demoralised the whole enemy party. He led yet another bayonet charge himself firing from his hip and accounted for two enemy in the bunker.
>
> On 18 March, during the advance on Jhangar, while attacking feature Ring Countour, he led his men with such skill that the enemy, though in a very commanding position, was thrown out and ran for life leaving behind a lot of equipment. He successfully captured a difficult

Operations in Jammu & Kashmir (1947-48)

objective without any loss of his platoon. In both these actions, this VCO's leadership, personal bravery, and utter fearlessness not only caused great damage to the enemy, but also proved a source of lasting inspiration to all the men in this unit. He worthily earned the respect of all ranks of his company".

The VrC was also awarded to another individual of the same name, albeit an NCO—Havildar Gurdial Singh. His citation reads:

"During attack on point 2916 (square 3102) in Jammu & Kashmir state, on 2 March 1948, he was commander of No 2 section of the leading platoon. The route top objective lay over a bare narrow spur to a pass some 300 yards below and then uphill another 300 yards all in full view of the enemy in well dug bunkers. His platoon had hardly advanced 30 yards when No 1 section was casualtied by an enemy mortar. Without looking back he pushed on to his objective and after going some 200 yards more came under accurate fire from hidden enemy position which both sections after short brilliant charge neutralized. This NCO was soon at the head of his section shouting war cries and firing accurately form hip with his sten gun, himself killing atleast one enemy.

From here onwards, it was an advance over a very naked spur to the enemy bunkers. His left forward group came under intense rifle and grenade fire from a well camouflaged bunker. He moved himself to the pinned down group and charged the bunker having thrown a grenade at it. The enemy threw a grenade at him shattering his right thigh completely. Two enemy, one rifle man and the other a swordsman counter attacked his left forward group. The rifleman was picked up by one of his groups and when the swordsman was about to deliver a blow, he rolled over to his side and killed him with his sten gun and thus saved his men from sure death. Although, severely wounded and profusely bleeding, he refused to be carried back and to be attended to until the objective was captured.

Right through this action, this NCO demonstrated leadership, individual bravery and toughness of a rare variety. He has made a name for himself and commands respect amongst the men for his outstanding conduct in that action."

Jhangar

The Patialas also played a prominent role in the recapture of Jhangar on 16-17 March 1948.

Brigadier Usman, commander 50 Para Brigade, was given the task to recapture Jhangar. He requested for making 1st Patiala available for the task. He used to consider 1st Patiala equal to two infantry battalions. The unit finally arrived in Naushera by end of February 1948 to form part of 50 Para Brigade for the recapture of Jhangar. Due to heavy rains in the area the plan for recapture of Jhangar was postponed several times. Then finally it materialized by mid March.

The battle of Jhangar and its subsequent recapture resulted in securing the lines of communications of troops in that sector, thereby paving the way for the liberation of Rajouri and subsequently towards the breaking of the siege of Punch.

The plan of 50 Para Brigade for the recapture of Jhangar entailed 7 Cavalry troop of Stuart tanks supported by one infantry battalion to advance along road Naushera – Jhangar

Operations in Jammu & Kashmir (1947-48)

and to clear the area towards Jhangar. 3 Maratha Light Infantry to secure Pirthil Nakka and 1st Patiala to thereafter advance to Jhangar. This plan was put into operation on 16 March 1948.

The advance was held up along the road as a 7 Cavalry Stuart tank was blown up by a powerful mine just northwest of Pirthil Nakka on the road. While the driver of the tank was killed other members of the crew suffered minor injuries. Progress of 3 Marathas for capture of Pirthil Nakka hill feature was also held up as the unit suffered two officers and 25 other ranks killed and two JCOs and 30 other ranks were wounded. Enemy was holding Pirthil Nakka with two companies supported by MMG platoon and two sections of 3" mortars.

1st Patiala was then summoned forward and a brigade attack was planned for the morning of 17 March. Orders for attack were given on the evening of 16 March. Air support was sought to support troops on call. A battery of a Field Regiment was to support the attack of each battalion and MMG sections were also made available to each battalion to provide fire support. While 3 Maratha was to capture the top of Pirthil Nakka from the right, 1st Patiala was to capture the middle feature of Pirthil Nakka left of 3 Maratha.

After the commanding officer of 1st Patiala gave out his orders to his 'O' group at about 4 p.m. on 16 March, the objectives were shown to the group. Following this, the commanders of the 'C' and 'D' assaulting companies, Major Shamsher Singh and Major Hazura Singh decided to take their respective platoons and section commanders and see the objective after dark from a point further up. Accordingly they moved out and it proved to be a difficult venture. They went towards the nullah below Pirthil Nakka and then started climbing up. When they were only 100 to 200 yards away from the enemy they quietly took up positions and soon heard noises of men walking around and probably cooking, since smell of the 'chapattis' being cooked was strong. As they moved a little aside they could hear some men talking, while some sentries were apparently smoking, since the smell of cigarettes was again quite strong. The party quietly slipped back and each company left behind one JCO and three NCOs as guides. They were fully armed with sten guns and grenades so that in case the enemy approached them they could fend for themselves. Before parting company the area of Forming Up Place (FUP) was also shown to them, which was just 200 yards to the rear. On their way back to the unit assembly area the party encountered a Maratha patrol, and had a narrow brush with the Marathas. But for some quick-witted identification drills the Patialas would have been in deep trouble.

As the two assaulting companies gathered their rations, ammunition and geared for moving out for the assault, the battalion headquarters started making preparations to move its tactical headquarters alongwith the two reserve companies, that is 'A' and 'B' companies.

At 5.15 a.m. 'C' and 'D' companies arrived at the FUP and met their respective JCOs and NCO guides. There was no communication with the Marathas. 'H' hour was 5.45 a.m. and the artillery, mortar and MMG rapid fire was to open up at 6 a.m. At 'H' hour the companies started moving up towards the enemy position, almost in one line, keeping one yard distance from man to man. When both the companies were within 200 yards of the enemy position, the Patialas heard sounds of utensils etc. emanating from the kitchen, and could smell the fresh meal being prepared.

Operations in Jammu & Kashmir (1947-48)

Suddenly all hell broke loose when fire support opened up. Nothing could be heard or seen in the din. When the fire stopped the attacking companies were just 75 to 100 yards from Top Spur. The Patialas assaulted shouting "Jo Bole So Nihal, Sat Sri Akal". Enemy troops were so completely taken up by surprise that they just ran for cover when both the companies stormed the position. Thereafter, without firing a single shot, they ran down the hill and vanished into the thin air.

3 Maratha, too, encountered a similar fate. Enemy had run away from their objective also. The Patiala casualty was only one other rank wounded, while enemy casualties included 10 killed and five captured. A large quantity of blankets and other warlike equipment was also recovered. Tea and cooked food to include rice, chapattis and meat were left in utensils, awaiting distribution to enemy troops who were not destined to consume the same.

At the daybreak, a sortie of IAF aircraft flew overhead and strafed the retreating enemy, which was about 1000 yards away from the captured objective. Due to thick undergrowth and forests the troops could not see anything beyond 200 yards. Thereafter the 'A' and 'B' reserve companies took on the advance and followed the retreating enemy. There was no enemy resistance right upto Jhangar, and Jhangar was recaptured the same evening. Both the assaulting battalions, that is 1st Patiala and 3 Maratha entered Jhangar almost simultaneously. Brigadier Usman arrived there that very evening, and the way was cleared for the capture of Rajauri and subsequent march towards Punch.

In this theatre, too, the unit earned a number of honours and awards. One such award was the MVC awarded to Sepoy Hari Singh whose qualifying act states:

"During the advance of Jhangar in Jammu & Kashmir state in an attack on Pirthil Nakka on 17 March 1948, Sepoy Hari Singh was a rifleman in the leading company. During the assault his section came under heavy fire and was pinned to the ground. He spotted an enemy bunker and after throwing a grenade rushed at it, firing his sten gun killing both the defenders. Another enemy bunker opened accurate fire on him. He was not deterred. Though wounded he killed one while the other fled. When the rest of his company came up, one enemy section led by an officer slipped away from a hidden post across his front. Sepoy Hari Singh was at least 20 yards ahead of his section and was responsible for killing the enemy officer.

By his individual actions, Sepoy Hari Singh was responsible for killing four enemies including an officer and breaking two enemy resistance points. In all these short but fierce actions where he could have lost his life any moment, he showed utter disrespect for intense and accurate enemy fire."

One officer and two NCOs also earned VrCs, namely, Major Joginder Singh, Naik Mehar Singh and Lance Naik Naurang Singh, the latter posthumously. Major Joginder Singh's qualifying act states:

"During an attack on a strong enemy position in Jammu & Kashmir on 2 March 1948, the whole of the leading section of the company commanded by Major Joginder Singh was wiped out by enemy 2 inch mortar. That did not deter him. He pushed another platoon, directed the show as if there were no enemy in front. He went forward and led a charge without losing any moment, killed and wounded 12 enemy soldiers at that spot. Men intoxicated by the good bag and having been inspired to a frenzy by their leader ran up the slopes to the bunker and delivered a cold blooded bayonet charge on the position and routed the enemy.

Again during the advance on Jhangar, he attacked the enemy with one automatic and a platoon and outmaneuvered the enemy. He enthused his troops with an indomitable will to win and the men followed him cheerfully giving their very best. Throughout this short and brilliant action, Major Joginder Singh exhibited outstanding courage and leadership".

Naik Mehar Singh's citation reads:

"During the advance on Jhangar and attack on Pirthil Nakka on 17 March 1948, Naik Mehar Singh was leading the right forward section. During the assault the enemy LMG and grenades came down on his section and wounded two of his men. He pushed on throwing grenades in front of him and charged the enemy and was the first on top and accounted for two enemy in trenches. Without waiting for the rest of the platoon to catch up, he charged with his men himself leading, all firing from hip and secured a foothold. By his initiative and action, he enabled his company to reach their objective without any further casualties to themselves. In both these actions, Naik Mehar Singh displayed outstanding initiative and daring which filled everyone in his company with enthusiasm and high spirits. Throughout the long hour of action, he set an example of leadership, tenacity of purpose and devotion to duty."

Lance Naik Naurang Singh's qualifying act states:

"During the attack on Pir Thil Nakka on 17 March 1948, Lance Naik Naurang Singh was commanding a section of the left forward platoon. A Browning and some riflemen were active on his front and the going was particularly difficult. He ordered the whole of his section to throw a grenade each and then he led an assault through an inferno of fire capturing the enemy post in a fast dash. He then pressed on to an enemy position in the rear which was still active, completely overrunning it without any loss to his men. At this stage another enemy post on the flank was spotted. After firing some rifle grenades at the post, he closed with it and destroyed it.

By these isolated individual actions on his own initiative, he gained for his company very advantageous ground which was responsible for routing the well-entrenched enemy in that sector. Throughout the action, he did not consider his own safety for a minute and exhibited fearless dash which made his men follow him cheerfully through very tough action".

After the battle of Jhangar the unit came back to Jammu on 27 March 1948 and was employed in the defence of Jammu and protection of line of communication. However, on 6 May 1948 the battalion was placed under command of 80 Infantry Brigade for a small action alongwith 1/2 Punjab involving the capture of a feature south of Seri, in the Naushera sector. On 7 May morning the unit took part in this operation and again showed its mettle to the enemy who suffered heavily, leaving behind four prisoners of war for the Patialas.

The Frozen Heights of Zojila

During this time situation in Kargil-Skardu areas deteriorated considerably and the enemy was literally

Operations in Jammu & Kashmir (1947-48)

reaching to occupy the strategic Zojila Pass, which was the only entrance into the valley from this direction.

By the evening of 8 May 1948, the unit returned to Jammu from Seri and, after some preparations, left for Sri Division on 10 May 1948. The unit reached Srinagar on 11 May 1948, and was despatched to Zojila Pass on 13 May 1948 under command of Lieutenant Colonel (later Brigadier) Sukhdev Singh VrC, MC. The move was necessitated to counter the enemy activities east of the Valley, while Sri Division launched a major offensive on the Muzzafarabad front.

Coming back to the east, the district of Ladakh, with its predominantly Budhist population, (although the Gilgit – Skardu – Kargil belt comprises a Shia Muslim majority population), was directly threatened after Pakistan had annexed the Skardu region of the state. Ladakh could only be reached either by the most difficult animal track from Manali or the somewhat more accessible route over the 11,000' high Zojila Pass linking Srinagar, the capital of the state of J&K to Leh, capital of J&K's remote high altitude district of Ladakh. After the outbreak of war, a military column had commenced the difficult trek from Manali to Leh in August 1948, but it would take considerable time to reach Leh. On the Zojila route, Pakistani troops and tribals had earlier captured Kargil on the other side of the Pass, and had also occupied its shoulders. By then it became apparent that the strategic Zojila Pass was under immense threat, being an objective of the highly trained Gilgit Scouts battalion of Pak army. They soon occupied dominating heights varying from 11,000 feet to 13,000 feet just behind and overlooking the Pass, apart from a few other smaller features near the Pass. Around this time the situation in the northern districts of Kargil-Skardu areas had deteriorated considerably and the enemy, which had broken through from there, was literally rushing to occupy the strategic Zojila Pass which was the only entrance into the Srinagar Valley from this northeasternly direction.

The approach to the Zojila Pass was guarded by a series of mountain ridges held by Pakistani troops, which had to be captured first to even get near the Pass. 77 Infantry Brigade under Brigadier K.L. Atal with 5 Maratha Light Infantry, 3 Jat and 1/5 Gurkha Rifles was tasked to force the Pass which the enemy was holding with Gilgit Scouts supported with Howitzers and 3 inch mortars. Their positions were located at heights of nearly 16000 feet, and they were making excellent use of natural caves overlooking the defile near the Pass. Codenamed 'Operation Duck', the first Indian attack in early September at the hitherto unattempted heights did not get far, as one of the battalions was held up by a glacier and another could not proceed in the face of intense enemy fire. The third attack from a different direction was also stalled. If the Pass was not taken soon, Leh would remain cut off throughout the winter, and it became necessary to find other ways to gain success.

Since the Zojila Pass and the approaches to it were well covered by machine gun fire of the enemy from the caves, it was decided that infantry troops in armoured personnel carriers and some tanks would offer the much needed cover to close up with the enemy positions, following which infantry columns would turn their flanks by mounting attacks on the high ranges. A squadron of Stuart tanks of 7 Cavalry alongwith some personnel carriers were moved 200 miles from Jammu. This was done in secrecy after the army workshops had removed the turrets of the tanks, to reduce their weight to suit the wooden bridges en-route, while improvised turrets were fitted onto the carriers so as to deceive the enemy into believing them to be tanks, and

Operations in Jammu & Kashmir (1947-48)

also to provide the requisite protection needed by the infantry while it closed up on the pass.

At this stage, on 18 June 1948, the then Prime Minister of India, Pandit Jawaharlal Nehru visited the unit at Sonamarg and was much impressed with the achievements of the unit. It was a historic day for all ranks of 1st Patiala Fierce fighting was still raging towards Zojila. When the Prime Minister insisted on being taken to the battle site, he was tactfully disuaded by the CO and Brigade Commander from going to the Zojila Pass. However, he was taken forward upto Baltal where he was given a comprehensive briefing of the operational situation. Impressed with the achievements of 1st Patiala, he personally requested the commanding officer to convey his high appreciation to all ranks on his behalf, and wished the Patialas good luck in their endeavour to capture Zojila. This blessing of the Prime Minister proved to be a great boon for the unit, as subsequent events unfurled. During May to November, the unit also earned numerous coveted awards.

This time the composition of 77 Brigade changed to include 4 Rajput, 1/5 Gurkha Rifles and 1 Patiala Infantry which were to launch the unusual attacks which had never been attempted in warfare earlier. 'D' Day was fixed for 20 October, after which heavy snow normally sets in to block the Pass. The Patialas, comprising cent percent, battle scarred Sikh troops, took on the challenge in spite of lack of proper equipment and training in high altitude warfare. In fact, the troops had never seen snow before.

The Zojila Pass at 11578 feet, is a little over 3 kilometres in length. The enemy had about battalion strength on the two shoulders dominating the Zojila defile, namely the Chabutra and Mukand ridges. While the Pass itself was in Indian hands, the enemy had occupied the features beyond it, upto 16000 feet. The battalion advanced towards Zojila but met with stiff resistance en route. First contact with the advancing enemy resulted in 21 Pak soldiers killed. Thereafter, for over a month, the raiders made incessant attempts to gain control of the dominating areas immediately around the Zojila Pass with a view to secure it, but every time the raiders were out-matched and out-fought by Indian troops. Innumerable deeds of outstanding gallantry were performed during this period of attrition. According to Lieutenant Colonel Sukhdev Singh, the commanding officer during this battle (later Brigadier), a classic example was the case of Naik Chet Singh who was holding a picquet with 13 men when attacked with mortars and machine guns. Eight of his jawans were wounded. He battled for seven hours with such extraordinary determination and skill that the raiders broke off the attack, leaving behind 36 of their own troops dead. Naik Chet Singh was subsequently awarded a VrC in this battle for his heroic act.

The new plan, due to the terrain not permitting any manoeuvres, was to attack frontally in the afternoon to seize the ridges dominating the defile. The Rajputs were to capture the Chabutra ridge on the left and the Gorkhas were to go for Mukand ridge on the right. The tanks were to support these attacks and, then advance with the Patialas to the Gumri basin on the far side of the Pass. However, due to inclement weather, which made tank movement impossible, the attack had to be postponed until 1 November, and for better luck 'Operation Duck' was changed to 'Operation Bison'.

While the Rajputs and Gurkhas assaulted their respective objectives as planned with determination and missionary zeal, thereby securing certain tactical footholds, the task of physically clearing the Pass fell on the Patialas, which were then known as 1st Patiala (Rajindra Sikh) Infantry.

Operations in Jammu & Kashmir (1947-48)

After some high altitude reconnaissance, it commenced its offensive on the night of 31 October/1 November 1948. During a severe snow-storm followed by a blizzard, when the temperature had dropped to minus 20 degrees, the determined Patialas toiled on hands and feet for six hours in the darkness and finally broke through the Pass and secured all surrounding heights between 13000' to 16000', thereby dominating the Pakistani positions.

Earlier during the night, a troop of tanks of 7 Cavalry, which had advanced along the mountainous road towards Zojila Pass, managed to secure its first objective just beyond the Pass – the Machoi defile, which had earlier been physically assaulted and captured by 4 Rajput. The enemy, surprised to see armour at this height and in such inclement weather, gave up its advantageous positions on the defile and fell back to take up positions behind the defile.

By first light on 1 November the Patialas started to roll down from the rear towards the enemy's well entrenched dug-in positions. On realizing that they were being surrounded, the Pakistani troops began to fall back, but were given a chase. The Patialas moved into the Gumri plain opposite the Machoi heights. In the extreme cold at 25 degrees below zero, the troops kept moving their limbs constantly to be warm and ready for the assault. The plan was to climb the snow covered rocky hills near the known enemy localities and launch a downhill attack at dawn. The companies laboured hard and moved using their hands and knees to climb the 1200 feet in six hours. Dawn saw the Patialas surprising the enemy from heights above the latter's position. The companies charged in, driving out the quilted enemy that were not already bayoneted. In this action, one of the Patiala's attacking companies located the enemy gun position and assaulted it with bayonets, killing most of its crew and capturing the remaining five men, including an intact 3.7 inch Pakistani Howitzer, the only prize of its kind in entire Jammu & Kashmir operations. This gun is now prominently displayed in the Quarter Guard of the battalion, which is now known as 15 Punjab (Patiala).

The weather, heavy snow and rugged terrain did not permit the 7 Cavalry armour to advance any further beyond the Machoi defile, which was still under enemy's observation and sporadic automatic fire. Due to poor visibility the Indian Air Force also could not support 7 Cavalry and 1st Patiala's successive operations.

The chase after Machoi was kept up by 4 Rajput but the advance was again held up at Matayan due to the enemy being in strong positions, as at Machoi. Nearby Batkundi, a precipitous and dominating feature, was particularly a strong position held by two companies supported by artillery and mortars. The support of artillery for the brigade attack was, thus, unavoidable. A road was, therefore, blasted into the hills by the engineers to bring forward guns and tanks, and this was achieved by 13 November.

The Patialas again came into the scene to secure the Batkundi feature, which covered the crossing over the river to Dras. The capture of Dras was a vital link in the operation to link up with Indian forces at Leh, and formation commanders were getting impatient at the delay. At this juncture the commanding officer of the 1st Patiala assured the Brigadier Atal that the Patialas would be in Dras on Guru Nanak's birth anniversary, which was scheduled on 16 November.

After a couple of days the Patialas launched another attack on the enemy, which had by now taken up defences much beyond Zojila and just 15 km short of Dras. Subsequently, in yet another night attack involving the crossing of a frozen river, and while constantly under fire,

Operations in Jammu & Kashmir (1947-48)

a small party of 20 men under Naib Subedar Lal Singh penetrated within 20 yards of the enemy defences and remained under constant but heavy small arms and automatic fire for the whole night. Inspite of being hit seven times, and in a semi-conscious state due to loss of blood, the Junior Commissioned Officer (JCO) remained at his post and directed accurate return fire on the enemy until the next morning when another party put in an attack, crushing the enemy defences and forcing his troops to withdraw. A good haul of weapons and ammunition was bagged. This JCO earned the coveted MVC in this battle.

On 15 November, the Patialas rushed the 20 odd kilometres to Dras clearing the areas of snipers and other opposition. The birthday of the Sikh Guru was celebrated by the troops in Dras and the civilians in the area observed that the goodwill and kindness of the Sikh troops contrasted greatly with the depredations caused by the enemy during their occupation. The entry of 1st Patiala in Dras marked the entry into the Ladakh region by Indian forces from Srinagar. The occasion was celebrated by Major General Thimayya hoisting the tricolour in Dras, cheered by a large crowd which had gathered to welcome him.

Next day two Patiala companies advanced towards Kargil while brushing aside minor opposition, despite the extreme cold and exhaustion, with its troops wading through freezing streams and mud slides. They reached Kargil on 23 November, and within a couple of days a successful link-up was established with Indian forces (2/8 Gorkha Rifles) advancing from Leh, thereby preventing the fall of Ladakh region into enemy hands.

In a period of less than three weeks following the Zojila battle, the surprised enemy was not only evicted with heavy casualties from his chain of strong defences under most trying winter conditions, but also an area of 2000 square miles was cleared of the enemy and the threat to Srinagar Valley from the east was removed once and for all.

In this theatre, too a number of individuals did exceptionally well during this battle, often performing even beyond the call of duty. Take the case of the rescue of a wounded soldier from the height of 15,500 feet, just below the enemy post 'Room'.

Sepoy Hardial Singh was a leading scout of a platoon which was sent at night to capture the enemy post 'Twin Pimples' held by 10 Gilgit Scouts. The post was to be captured just before the first light. The platoon halted briefly to recover its breath when Sepoy Hardial Singh came within 10 yards of an enemy LMG bunker. Just then someone from the leading section coughed which alerted the enemy and invited LMG fire in small bursts. Sepoy Hardial Singh was hit in the right lung and he rolled down 30 yards onto an inaccessible ledge of ice. While under enemy fire the platoon moved back and did not return fire. The platoon commander returned to Goohar Valley and reported that Sepoy Hardial Singh was dead, which was not so.

The enemy post could not see the wounded soldier lying below, so no further fire was opened up on him, but normal fire continued between the Patiala post 'Shoulder' and enemy post 'Twin Pimples'. However, the same platoon was directed to return in the evening and bring back Sepoy Hardial Singh dead of alive. Two local coolies, who had volunteered to accompany the platoon, were also sent with it. Representatives of pioneer platoon with ropes and ladders were also sent with the platoon, which arrived in the area at about 10 p.m.

One coolie named Mohammad Ismail moved forward with hopes to reach Sepoys Hardial Singh's position, after

Operations in Jammu & Kashmir (1947-48)

which two more NCOs and three sepoys were lowered along with ladders. The injured sepoy was thereafter strapped with a turban on the back of Mohammad Ismail and lifted from the ledge with the help of ropes and ladders. He was brought down to Goohar with a big opening in the right lung. He was then put on a stretcher and carried to Baltal where he was given first aid and rushed to the military hospital at Srinagar. After a prolonged operation Sepoy Hardial survived. The story goes that the surgeon who operated on him ordered that the patient should not be given anything to eat or drink for the next twenty-four hours. Captain Sucha Singh, the unit intelligence officer (IO), went to look him up the next morning at 10 a.m. To his utter surprise he found Hardial, though lying in bed covered with a blanket, drinking rum and eating meat in gravy. Sucha asked him as to why he was doing this when it was prohibited by the surgeon. Promptly the sepoy replied - "Sahib, when I did not die in that difficult terrain where I remained lying injured and without food, I do not visualize dying with rum and meat in gravy now."

Incidentally Mohammad Ismail, the civilian porter employed by 1st Patiala and 3 Jat during this war earned the coveted MVC. He is the only civilian to receive this award. His citation reads:

> "On 23 June 1948, in the Zojila Pass area in Jammu & Kashmir, a reconnaissance patrol was ambushed and a man was severely wounded. He rolled down the side of the hill, and was unable to get back to the picquet. All attempts by the section to recover the wounded man failed as the enemy had covered the area with fire. Ismail, who was a civilian labourer, volunteered to bring in the wounded man single-handed. He displayed outstanding skill in negotiating the almost impassable snow covered slopes swept

by MMG fire. By superb physical effort he got the wounded man, bundled him up in his blanket and brought him to safety.

Again on 14 September 1948, at Zojila Pass during an attack by 3 Jat, Ismail volunteered to accompany that unit as a guide. Advancing with the leading scouts in spite of close and continuous fire he guided the troops and it was only when a hidden MMG had wiped out the leading line that he fell into enemy hands and became a prisoner. On both occasions, Ismail displayed bravery, devotion to duty and disregarded for personal safety".

In this theatre the other MVCs awardees included Jemadar Sampuran Singh, Jemadar Hardev Singh (posthumously), Naik Pritam Singh (posthumously) and Sepoy Amar Singh. Amongst the VrCs awardees were Subedar Sant Singh (posthumously), Naib Subedar Balwant Singh, Havildar Singh Mukand Singh, Lance Naik Sajjan Singh and Lance Naik Chand Singh (both posthumously), sepoys Gajjan Singh, Hazura Singh, Zaila Singh, Teja Singh (all posthumously) and Sepoy Bachan Singh.

The brief qualifying acts of the MVC awardees goes thus:

Jemadar Sampooran Singh:

"At Gumri in Jammu & Kashmir, Jemadar Sampooran Singh was in command of a platoon picquet. The enemy attacked this picquet with two companies supported by two 4.2/3.7 guns, two 3 inch mortars, three MMGs, five Browning and three 2 inch mortars. The enemy reached within about 200 yards of an outpost which was the key position to the picquet.

Appreciating the critical situation, this JCO rushed forward with a couple of men to the outpost crossing

Operations in Jammu & Kashmir (1947-48)

some 80 yards of heavily blitzed area, without giving the slightest thought to personal safety. His presence there infused the men with invincible effort. The enemy after a break of about an hour put in a very big fire attack which was completely defeated. Four hours later, the enemy launched his biggest attack only to be pushed back with heavier losses. With sheer guts and determination, Jemadar Sampooran Singh completely overwhelmed the superior enemy causing him at least 60 casualties.

This JCO showed most inspiring leadership and indomitable courage over a long period under most trying conditions, commanding complete confidence of the men under his command".

Jemadar Hardev Singh, MVC (posthumous):

"At Machhoi in Jammu & Kashmir state, Jemadar Hardev Singh was in command of a platoon patrol. His platoon was heavily engaged by intense, accurate and close fire, killing or wounding a third of his men. He himself was wounded in the arm. Realising the seriousness of the situation, he moved in heavy snow covered area from man to man through a hail of automatic and mortar fire trying to collect his party to the hillside from where he could keep the enemy engaged till reinforcements came. In this process he was twice hit in the shoulder but this JCO's indomitable to beat the enemy.

Gravely disregarding his personal safety he got all his wounded men to the nearest cover. He was the last man to crawl back to cover and while doing so he was mortally wounded by an MMG burst. He refused to be attended to until all his wounded men had been provided with medical aid and dressed up.

Before succumbing to his injuries, he properly organised and enthused his men to put up determined resistance against the enemy. This JCO displayed gallantry, grit and calmness of the highest degree. He lived up to the highest traditions of his unit."

Naik Pritam Singh, MVC (posthumously):

"At Gumri in Jammu & Kashmir state, Naik Pritam Singh was in charge of a signal detachment when enemy shelling cut all line communications and made movement impossible. He volunteered to go out and repair the lines. He moved out with cool determination, completely unperturbed by shells busting all around him and heavy enemy MMG fire directed on him. Escaping sure death right under the nose of the enemy, he mended the wires and got back under the hail of MMG fire having seen the line through. He repeated the ordeal through heavy fire twice in the afternoon. Once he repaired the line to another picquet and next he replaced a broken-down wireless set of yet another picquet.

This NCO showed exemplary fortitude, courage and devotion to duty throughout the nerve-shattering and most trying operations. His fearless and tenacious conduct filled everyone in the unit with great inspiration and admiration for him."

Sepoy Amar Singh, MVC:

"At Zojila Pass in Jammu & Kashmir, Sepoy Amar Singh was LMG No 1 in a listening post. At 6.10 am the enemy opened intense fire with all his weapons on the picquet position followed by an advance. A third of the picquet was

Operations in Jammu & Kashmir (1947-48)

destroyed and Amar Singh, wounded severely in the head, lay semi-conscious while his No 2 had his arms shattered. The enemy made fanatical but abortive attempts to rush the picquet. But Amar Singh kept on firing signal shots and occasional short bursts accurately, thus holding the enemy at bay single handed. Throughout the day, enemy guns did not stop for a moment and some 200 enemy kept shouting and yelling at him. But this young soldier kept his head, firing eleven magazines out of the sixteen he had during the course of over 5 hours and still keeping reserve the five magazines for hand-to-hand fight.

The picquet was reinforced in the afternoon. Though he was profusely bleeding and feeling faint from the skull injury, he held on completely defying the heavy odds against him and utterly disregarding sure annihilation. He was carried inside at 10 p.m. still full of fight and determination to beat back the enemy. Throughout the sixteen hours of battle, this sepoy displayed extreme coolness of mind, skill in use of weapons and courage."

The brief qualifying acts of the remaining VrCs awardees are given below:

Subedar Sant Singh, VrC (posthumous):

"At Machhoi in Jammu & Kashmir on, while attacking a feature, Jemadar Sant Singh was in command of a leading platoon. The advance lay over 2,000 yards of heavily snow covered ground in full view of the enemy. Any outflanking move was out of question because of heavy snow and sheer climb. Right from the start line, his platoon came under MMG fire halting the advance. He kept moving from section to section inspiring his men to carry on without caring for personal safety. His men responded promptly and unfalteringly.

He continued with the assault till 8 p.m. under heavy fire with himself in the frontline with such dash that the enemy fled leaving behind 12 dead. His fearless and vigorous drive contributed chiefly to the success of the attack. In this long and difficult action, Jemadar Sant Singh showed leadership, courage and tenacity of purpose of a high calibre."

Naib Subedar Balwant Singh, VrC:

"On the night of 1 November 1948, at the Zojila Pass in Jammu & Kashmir, Jemadar Balwant Singh was in command of a platoon detailed to bypass an enemy post and occupy a hill feature adjacent to it. There was 200 yards of detour, involving climbing on heavily snow covered hills in close proximity to the enemy. But Jemadar Balwant Singh, without caring for darkness and snow that stood in his way, reached the top of the hill in four hours and encircled on enemy post hardly 200 yards below.

With his platoon he lay there for the whole night and at dawn, realising that the enemy was hiding below in curved caves and might escape, he did not wait for orders, took out two sections and systematically charged one cave after another with automatics, rifles and hand grenades. He combed out the whole area, inflicted many casualties on the enemy and captured one 3.7 gun, one Bren gun, two rifles and vast quantities of equipment. Throughout this vital engagement, Jemadar Balwant Singh displayed consistent superb courage, utter fearlessness and a most invigorating leadership."

Operations in Jammu & Kashmir (1947-48)

Havildar Mukand Singh, VrC:

"On 4 November 1948 at Zojila Pass, Havildar Mukand Singh was a platoon havildar of the company detailed to destroy an enemy resistance pocket. He manoeuvred round the enemy position, while the rest of his platoon gave covering fire. Every inch of a distance of about 200 yards from the enemy position was covered by heavy enemy automatic fire. This brave NCO was the leading man of the section and by his dauntless action persuaded every man to follow him fearlessly over the area heavily swept by enemy fire. Two of his men were seriously wounded. Leading the five remaining men, he blitzed the enemy position with grenades, killing five of the enemy and capturing two. In addition he captured a Bren gun, a collection of arms and a large quantity of ammunition equipment and documents.

Throughout this operation, Havildar Mukand Singh showed leadership, courage and determination of a very high order."

Lance Naik Sajjan Singh, VrC (posthumous):

"At Machhoi in Jammu & Kashmir, while attacking a feature, Lance Naik Sajjan Singh was in command of a forward section platoon. During the assault his section was subjected to particularly heavy fire from enemy 2 inch mortars and grenades, killing two of his men and temporarily halting his section. He went from man to the other, cheering and directing them, taking no notice whatever of the intense fire all round him, filling his men with complete confidence and air of superiority.

From here, with himself leading, he blitzed the enemy position and was responsible for killing two with his sten gun and grenade. All through the action by his utter fearlessness and disregard for his personal safety, he made the men willingly go through a terribly tough and dangerous time and was always in complete control of the situation. This NCO exhibited leadership, courage and vigorous dash which command spontaneous respect from his men."

Lance Naik Chand Singh, VrC (posthumously):

"On 3 May 1948, Lance Naik Chand Singh was in command of the leading section of a patrol at Machhoi. His platoon came under heavy and accurate MMG and automatic fire, killing and wounding half of his section straightaway. He collected the LMG and 2 inch mortar bomb (to be used as grenades) from his killed comrades with a view to reorganizing his section and containing the enemy to prevent him from taking away our casualties. From about 12 noon to about 5.30 p.m., when reinforcement arrived, he so directed the fire of his party that the enemy, in spite of continuous and frantic efforts, was unable to move.

The enemy concentrated all his efforts on the NCO's little hideout causing two casualties to his party of five. But he held on. At 5.30 p.m. when an attack was put in by his company on the enemy occupied hill feature, he got out of his hideout with his party and joined the battle, silencing an enemy sniper post. This superb gallant action of Naik Chand Singh was largely responsible for saving nine of his comrades and the whole of his platoon equipment.

In an all-day battle, he displayed the highest soldierly qualities of leadership, personal bravery and selfless devotion to duty."

Sepoy Gajjan Singh, VrC (posthumous):

"At Zojila Pass, Sepoy Gajjan Singh was Bren Gun No 1. After stand down, he was away from his position when the enemy opened up heavy MMG and LMG fire on the picquet. He rushed back to the picquet position under very accurate and close fire to man his LMG and was hit in the leg. Undeterred by his wound and determined to reach his LMG, he crawled forward in full view of the enemy not caring for his personal safety.

Having got his LMG he was not satisfied with his position and crept forward to another place and was again hit in the shoulder, but managed to engage the enemy from his new position. His well-aimed fire was responsible for killing and wounding at least five enemy and temporarily slowing down the enemy attack. At this stage he was caught by an MMG burst, mortally wounding him."

"Sepoy Teja Singh was wireless operator of a section picquet at Machhoi when the enemy put an attack. A direct mortar hit put his set out of commission and he got wounded in his left arm. There being no other communication with the commander, this signaler volunteered to go out some 300 yards to the main telephone line with his telephone to pass information to the commander. He moved out in full view of the enemy and under intense enemy MMG fire. He was again hit in the thigh but managed to tap the line and send the message.

Then he dashed back to join the battle, although bleeding heavily. When only some 20 yards from the picquet he was hit by an MMG burst in the chest and died. This young signaler displayed supreme courage and determination in carrying out his duties."

Sepoy Hazura Singh, VrC (posthumous):

"At Gumri in Jammu & Kashmir state, Sepoy Hazura Singh was doing LMG No 1 duty in a section outpost. The enemy put in a two company attack supported by mortars and MMGs and managed to reach within 200 yards of the outpost. Although head covers and stone 'sangars' had collapsed because of enemy mortar fire, he fired his weapon with extreme accuracy, causing serious losses to the enemy. He thus became the chief target for all enemy weapons. Though wounded in the left shoulder, he kept on using his weapon with deadly effect.

The enemy, unable to over-run this outpost, tried a small detour. On his own initiative, Hazura Singh crawled some 15 yards to a new advantageous position but was hit again in his leg and thigh. Although feeling feeble from profuse bleeding he kept on engaging the enemy with great skill and accuracy, halting the new enemy move. He was caught by an MMG burst in the head, which killed him instantaneously. In making the supreme sacrifice, Sepoy Hazura Singh by his outstanding courage and skill at arms, caused heavy losses to the enemy, definitely breaking the tempo of the enemy attack."

Sepoy Zaila Singh, VrC (posthumous):

"At Gumri in Jammu & Kashmir, Sepoy Zaila Singh was No 2 of an LMG outpost. At 6 am the enemy attacked the picquet with two companies with MMG and 2 inch mortar support and reached some 400 yards. As his LMG No 1 got seriously wounded, Sepoy Zaila Singh at once took over the gun, killing or wounding at least three enemy.

Under barrage of 2 inch mortar and heavy concentration of MMG cross fire, the enemy advanced to within 200 yards of this outposts but Zaila Singh used his weapon with such devastating effect that the advance of the enemy was temporarily halted. His picquet commander shouted at him to crawl back to the main position. But knowing that he was causing heavy losses to the enemy, he stuck to his position saying that he was more useful there. The enemy, unable to advance without overrunning this outpost, furiously engaged this one man outpost with all the weapons he had, mortally wounding Sepoy Zaila Singh. This brave man by his selfless gallant stand and devotion to duty and his individual skilful action forced the enemy to temporarily abandon an attack on the picquet. He made the supreme sacrifice for the safety of his comrades."

Sepoy Bachan Singh, VrC:

"At Machhoi in Jammu & Kashmir on Sepoy Bachan Singh was a rifleman in the leading section of a platoon which was heavily engaged by enemy MMG and LMG fire from a hill feature. He was hit by a burst in the leg shattering it completely. By skilful fieldcraft and sheer guts he dragged himself a distance of 300 yards to where his section commander had signalled him. All the way to his place he was constantly under close automatic fire missing him by inches. This did not deter this tough and tenacious soldier from carrying on to join his section.

Having joined the section after a little dressing, he volunteered to be allowed to fire his rifle, although he was feeling very weak from loss of blood. He kept on shooting for over eight hours lying on one side only till he was carried back. His personal valour and dogged determination, while being very seriously wounded, set an inspiring example for his comrades."

The *Indian News Chronicle* of 18 June 1948 recorded the gallantry of Lance Naik Chand Singh of 1st Patiala in the following words:

"Sikh NCO's Gallantry on Kashmir Front." Srinagar, June 17,– "A Sikh non-commissioned officer Lance Naik Chand Singh, 1st Patiala Infantry, played an outstanding part in an action which was fought recently on a 12,000 feet high hill feature, North East of Sonamarg. The incident occurred when a platoon of Sikhs was sent on patrol with the object of finding out whether a certain bridge in the vicinity was intact. The hill area was covered with about 6 feet deep snow and any movement against the open background was within the raider's view.

When our patrol approached their objective, the raiders, who were found to be occupying a dominating hill feature, opened fire with medium machine guns, light machine guns and two-inch mortars. Our patrol, owing to lack of cover, suffered some casualties.

Lance Naik Chand Singh with five others managed to crawl into a crevice and from that position brought intensive fire to bear on the raiders which foiled their efforts to take away our casualties and weapons. The raiders thus were kept engaged for over five hours until four platoons of Jammu and Kashmir Infantry and Patiala Infantry came to their rescue.

The raiders positions were then over run and they fled leaving behind 21 dead, two rifles, 2,785 rounds of small arms ammunition, 24 blankets and some utensils."

Operations in Jammu & Kashmir (1947-48)

The story of Havildar Mukand Singh was described by *The Hindustan Times* dated 20 November 1948 through prominent headlines: "Fought for 3 days Without Food". Datelined Zojila, November 16, the news item reads:

"The story of how a 17,000 feet range on Zojila, came to be named after Havildar Mukand Singh of Patiala, is recounted by an Army Observer with our forward troops in Kashmir.

The ridge, which holds a dominating position in Zojila, was secured by Indian troops within two hours from the launching of an offensive in this sector on the morning of November 1.

Wounded and alone on the ridge, this gallant soldier kept 200 raiders at bay for three days with his Bren gun until he became unconscious from sheer exhaustion and loss of blood.

Havildar Mukand Singh, whom the observer met at Machhoi, seven miles from Zojila on November 3, gave the following of how he held the enemy beyond the pass for three days:

"When the enemy overwhelmed my platoon on July 3, I had to fall back on Zojila with 13 of my men. I took up a position high on the right of the ridge and sent out my men to take up positions on the left ridge, which is known as Chhabutra Hill, and was given this name as the top of the hill, as you see now, was then completely covered with snow and gave the appearance of a platform.

With my few men I had to fight off an enemy about 200 in number but we did not lose heart. Though I was injured in my right arm, I had plenty of Bren gun ammunition and I kept firing my gun at the enemy with my left hand, and prevented their advance for three days. As I had no food or rest for three days, I got fainter and fainter and then lost consciousness. I later found myself in a hospital."

Major General K.S. Thimayya, the GOC of Sri (later Srinagar) Division published a Special Order of the Day prior to the move of the unit to Patiala. It said:

"This is to bid farewell to you officers and men of the 1st Battalion the Patiala Regiment on the eve of your departure to Patiala. After the outbreak of hostilities, your battalion was the first unit to arrive in Jammu on 3 November 1947. From then, till you arrived in the Kashmir valley, you formed part of JAK Forces in which you played an outstanding part in combating the enemy's depredations into state territory and enhanced your reputation as a fine fighting unit.

On 12 May 1948 you entered the Kashmir valley to form part of my Division. From the very day you arrived I allotted you an independent task which was to prevent the enemy from penetrating into the Kashmir valley through the Zojila Pass. This task was a vital one as the remainder of the Division was involved in a major offensive in the west. At that time you had no artillery support. The country in which you operated was covered in snow, the climate was intensely cold and the terrain was mountainous and treacherous. For five months you fought an enemy which outnumbered you by 3 to 1 and who was a tough and fanatical fighter, but you carried out the task given to you to my entire satisfaction.

Every hill and every nullah in the Zojila area will always echo with the deeds of bravery performed by you all. Then in November 1948 you formed

Operations in Jammu & Kashmir (1947-48)

part of 77 Para Brigade, which took on the offensive, driving the enemy out of Zojila. You were also responsible for the capture of Dras and Kargil, thus saving the Ladakh valley and Leh. This is a fine ending to your 13 months of campaigning in the Kashmir operations.

During these operations you suffered the following casualties:

	Killed	**Wounded**
Officers	-	1
JCOs 1	2	
ORs	22	62

You inflicted the following casualties upon the enemy:

Killed	**Wounded**	**Captured**
234	464	17 Prisoners

You captured the following arms and equipment from the enemy:

3.7 Howitzer	-	1
Bren Guns	-	3
Rifles	-	31
Pistols Sigs	-	2 and plenty of kit, equipment and stores.

You had built up a great reputation as a fighting battalion in World War II and in these Kashmir operations you have further enhanced this. I have been very proud to have you in my Division and it is with a sad heart that I bid farewell to you officers and men whom I have come to love and admire. You have helped to lay the foundation of this new

Division and build up its reputation. You have kept the dignity and reputation of your Ruler, H.H. the Maharaja who sent you, and I know he will be proud to hear of your valiant deeds.

I wish each one of you a good and well earned rest and may God be with you. Jai Hind".

In another letter No. 1072 dated 17 December 1948 written by Lieutenant General KM Cariappa, to the Commanding Officer 1st Patiala, Lieutenant Colonel Sukhdev Singh, VrC, MC, it is stated:

"I write this to congratulate you and all others under your command in that magnificent battalion of yours very much on the splendid show you put up in Jammu & Kashmir in the year you were there. It was always such a joy to come and see your unit, to meet you, your officers and men, to find such excellent morale, good fellowship and efficiency all round. I know you have not only served as very excellent soldiers, but you have also done your humanitarian duties in looking after the unfortunate local population, wherever you went, who had been harrased and hounded by the hostiles. I thank you all not only for your very good service under your command, but also for your excellent hospitality whenever I visited your unit.

I am sorry you are leaving 5 Corps, but I do know how well you deserve a rest after your long and arduous time there under trying conditions.

Wishing you all the very best of luck always."

In this battle numerous honours and awards were also won by various other battalions which participated in this theatre. As a matter of fact, separate chapters or articles could be written on the valorous conduct of the other battalions as well, including 7 Cavalry. However, the Patialas, who had already shown their mettle earlier in the battles of Chhamb, Naushera and Jhangar prior to the battle of Zojila, established an enviable record during this war. It won a total tally of 8 MVCs, 18 VrCs (to include one which was awarded to the CO himself) and various other awards as well, including the coveted battle honour–'Zojila'. This is an unparallelled record to have been established by a battalion during any war in the history of Indian army.

The battalion moved to Jammu in late December to become the corps reserved, and after the cease-fire on 1 January 1949, it received orders to prepare for moving back to Patiala.

THE POST INDEPENDENCE PERIOD

Defence Minister Shri Baldev Singh with officers of 1st Patiala before the Zojila operations -1948

1st Patiala ammunition column advancing towards Zojila

Prime Minister Pandit Jawaharlal Nehru being briefed on the Zojila operations by the Commanding Officer, Lieutenant Colonel Sukhdev Singh, MC

Prime Minister Pandit Jawaharlal Nehru inspecting troops of 1st Patiala in Kashmir after the famous battle of Zojila-1948

IN JAMMU & KASHMIR

Honourable Sheikh Abdullah, the Prime Minister of J&K, presenting a shield to CO 1st Patiala at the Polo Ground, Srinagar, for the unit's outstanding service to the state - 8 August 1948

Sheikh Abdullah, the Prime Minister of J & K, with officers of 1st Patiala Infantry-1948

Prime Minister of India, Pandit Jawaharlal Nehru visits
1st Patiala at Baltal, J&K -1948
(Also seen in the photo are the Defence Minister of India,
Shri Baldev Singh; LT Gen Kulwant Singh and
CO, LT Col Sukhdev Singh MC, (centre) with other
dignitaries, officers and men of 1st Patiala

Major General K S Thimayya, GOC Kashmir Division, inspects
the unit on completion of its active
operational service in J&K - 9 December 1948

THE HEROES OF ZOJILA

Winners of MVC - Zojila - 48 *(Left to Right -Top Row)*
Sub Gurdial Singh, Jem Sampooran Singh,
Jem Hardev Singh, Jem Lal Singh, Nk Pritam Singh,
Sep Amar Singh, and Sep Hari Singh
Winners of VrC - Zojila-48 *(From Middle Row - Left)*
Brig Sukhdev Singh, MC, Sub Sant Singh, Jem Balwant
Singh, L/Hav Phuman Singh, Hav Mukand Singh,
Hav Chet Singh, Nk Mehar Singh, L/Nk Sajjan Singh,
L/Nk Chand Singh, Sep Zaila Singh and Sep Bachan Singh

On return to Patiala state
after the J&K operations.*

*(Photos courtesy Maj Gen C S Brar, son of Capt (later Col) D S Brar of 1st Patiala Lancers & 62 Cav)

Officers and men of 1st Patiala on their return to Patiala state after the J&K operations.*

*(Photos courtesy Maj Gen C S Brar, son of Capt (later Col) D S Brar of 1st Patiala Lancers & 62 Cav)

Area of Zoji La-1948

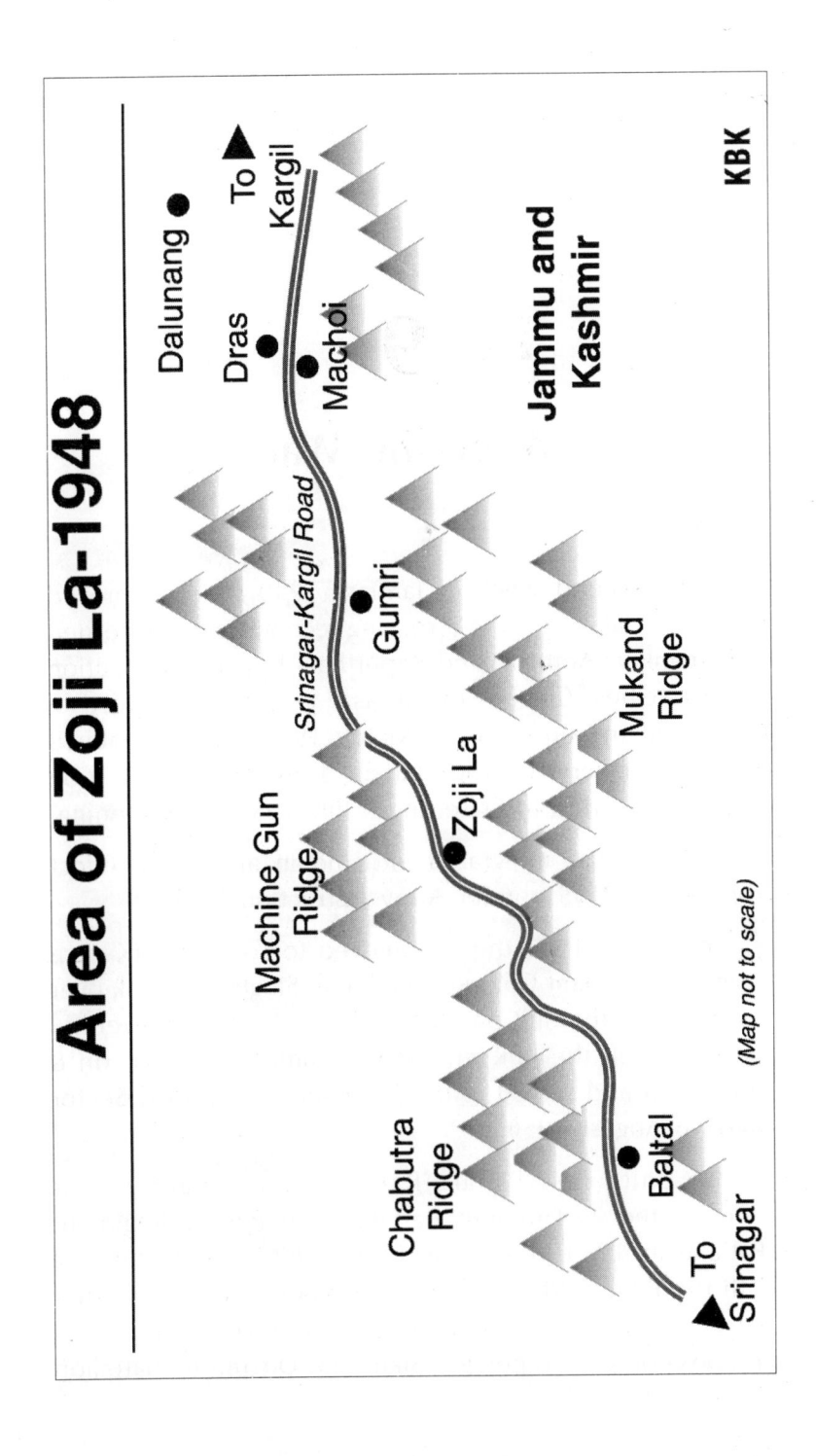

(Map not to scale)

Jammu and Kashmir

KBK

9

After the War

In the second week of January 1949 the unit moved back to Patiala. En route a rousing reception was accorded at Pathankot, Amritsar and Kapurthala by local population of these cities. Citizens of Amritsar presented a Sword of Honour to the unit. On 10 March 1950, the unit moved ex-State for services with Indian army in concentration area and reverted to State on 27 July 1950, for screening.

The unit was integrated into Indian army with effect from 1 April 1951 under Army Instruction 12/S/50.

On 17 July 1951 the unit moved to Yol Camp (Kangra Valley). Lieutenant Colonel Gurcharan Singh, MC took over command of the unit on 15 March 1952. After an eventful tenure at Yol, the unit moved to Jammu & Kashmir on 8 April 1953 and served in the 25 Infantry Divisional Sector upto 16 August 1956.

The unit (First Patiala Rajindra Sikh Infantry) was redesignated as Fifteenth Battalion the Punjab Regiment (Patiala) in 1954 vide Army Order 363/54 and affiliated with the Punjab Regiment for all purposes. Whereas other battalions of the Punjab Regiment have mixed class composition of 100 percent Sikhs and Dogra, the battalion retained its original class composition of 100 percent Sikhs. Lieutenant Colonel VS Yog took over from Lieutenant Colonel Gurcharan Singh, MC on 18 October 1955 and continued to command the battalion for more than four and a half years.

From Jammu & Kashmir the unit moved to Dagshai and served in the 4 Infantry Divisional Sector upto 12 May 1959. During its stay in this sector extensive training was carried out and the unit had the honour of staging a demonstration of a 'Battalion in Attack' for the visiting Chinese delegation alongwith the Staff College candidates in 1958 during 'Exercise Aag'. In this demonstration all the 3" mortars of the formation were brigaded and the assaulting troops were supported by brigaded mortars, artillery, armour and a squadron of fighter aircraft. The exercise was extremely well conducted and came in for tremendous praise from various quarters.

The unit once again moved to Jammu & Kashmir, where it operated in high altitude and snow bound areas of Tangdhar from 13 May 1959 to 19 September 1962. It was orbated to 401 Infantry Brigade of 19 Infantry Division. In December 1960 the command of the battalion devolved on Lieutenant Colonel J.S. Mandher who commanded for three years. His adjutant was Captain (later Colonel) PS Vasudevan. The unit proved its mettle in operations, sports and adventure activities, and also had the unique distinction of winning the Divisional Shooting Championship for four consecutive years during its stint with the formation. As per traditions the Patialas were permitted to retain the trophy, which is proudly displayed in the unit officer's mess till date. The unit's strong winter patrol which successfully crossed the famous Nasta Chun Pass, a totally snow covered pass between Kupwara and Tangdhar, became a legendary event which was remembered by the unit and the formation for many years to come. After its tenure in the valley the unit moved to Barrackpore.

During the Chinese aggression the unit was airlifted to Sikkim on 27 October 1962, having hardly spent one month in Barrackpore. At Sikkim defensive positions were established by the unit in record time at the height of 14,000 feet. This feat was highly appreciated by various commanders up the chain.

It was only due to the extremely high standard of the unit's fighting ability and level of training that it was selected to be the Divisional Mobile Reserve of 20 Infantry Division in 1963. Lieutenant Colonel (later Major General, now retired) H.S. Kullar took over the command of the Patialas on 11 September 1963.

The Patialas moved to Calcutta in connection with Internal Security duties in January 1964, and was stationed at Barrackpore, under Headquarters Bengal Area. On termination of Internal Security duties in March 1964 the unit reverted to its parent formation.

Thereafter the unit, alongwith other units of 32 Mountain Brigade, was placed under command 9 Mountain Division from 30 April 1965 to 10 August 1966. During this period the unit took part in 'Op Ablaze' and 'Op Riddle'. On 15 June 1966, Lieutenant Colonel C.S. Dosanj, took over the command of the battalion.

On 11 August 1966 the unit moved to Ladakh where it was placed under command 70 Infantry Brigade. Having excelled in the battle of Zojila, the troops felt quite 'at home' in the familiar surroundings. Here again the unit gave a good account of itself for two years, facing cheerfully all the hazards of high altitude and temperatures as low as minus 42° C.

After the War

Lieutenant Colonel J.S. Sandhu (later Brigadier) took over command on 27 May 1968. On completion of its high altitude tenure the unit moved to serve under 80 Infantry Brigade from 27 July 1968 to 22 September 1969. This was an area familiar to the Patialas, having fought the famous battle of Naushera and Jhangar in this sector.

During this new stint, the unit was committed operationally throughout its stay in this sector, and had the honour of manning the same picquets which it had captured in 1948. The unit, alongwith other battalions of the Punjab Regiment received new colours on 18 March 1969 at Meerut in the presence of five former commanding officers of the battalion, including Lieutenant General Balwant Singh. The colours were presented at an impressive colour presentation ceremony organised by the Punjab Regimental Centre, and President Zakir Hussain presented the new colours to the battalions.

The unit moved to Ferozepore in September 1969 and was placed under command 29 Infantry Brigade. While at Ferozepore it did extremely well in training, games and sports. Lieutenant Colonel G.B.V.L. Sastry took over command during 16 August 1970. It was during his tenure that the battalion participated in the 1971 Indo-Pak war.

10

Indo-Pak War – 1971

Before describing the conduct of the Patialas during this war, it will be pertinent to mention the causes leading to the war.

The events that led to the birth of Bangladesh in 1971 are common knowledge. The trouble had its roots in the partition of the Indian sub-continent, which created Pakistan with its two wings – East Pakistan and West Pakistan. These wings were 1,600 kilometres apart and, except for their religion, the two people had hardly anything in common. The Bengalis of East Pakistan differed from the West Pakistanis in their customs, food habits, dress and, above all, language. Though the eastern wing was larger in population, it was ruled from West Pakistan; and one of the main grouses of the people of East Pakistan was that adequate attention was not paid to its development. All this created a demand for autonomy.

The result of the December 1970 general elections was a decisive victory for Sheikh Mujibur Rahman, leader of the Awami League, a party that sought autonomy for East Pakistan. Surprised by the election results, the Pakistani military rulers tried to persuade the Sheikh to cut down his demands. When he refused martial law was imposed in

Indo-Pak War – 1971

East Pakistan. The Bengalis were furious and the Sheikh reacted by launching a civil disobedience movement. This brought General Yahya Khan for talks to Dacca, East Pakistan's capital. When the talks failed he departed, leaving the task of suppressing the movement for autonomy to the Pakistan Army.

Events thereafter moved fast. The Sheikh was arrested on 25 March and flown to West Pakistan, while East Pakistanis launched a massive protest. The resultant crackdown by Pakistan army was ruthless and its actions assumed an aspect of great brutality. Soon more and more troops were flown into East Pakistan to further suppress the uprising. After carrying out a genocide of nearly one million people, a flood of refugees surged into India. By November nearly twelve million Bangladeshi refugees were on Indian soil and the influx imposed an intolerable burden upon India. Thus, Pakistan had created a situation in East Pakistan which threatened India's security. When India protested to Pakistan and simultaneously appealed to the international community for assistance, Pakistan became more and more belligerent towards India and its Air Force attacked a number of Indian bases by first light on 3 December 1971. Indian immediately retaliated and war was declared that day.

India had no option but to liberate East Pakistan with the active support of its local people. In this theatre many Indian formations and units fought the war, code named 'Op Cactus Lilly', while many battles proved to be decisive subsequently.

At the Western Sector

In the wake of President Yahya Khan's threats, India had considered the myriad of courses open to Pakistan on the Western front. Many possibilities were considered such as an attack across the cease-fire line in the hilly areas of Jammu & Kashmir, or attacks even in the Chhamb, Samba-Jammu or Samba-Pathankot sub sectors. An offensive in the Punjab plains and forays into Rajasthan were also envisaged. However, due to the commitment on the eastern front and the possibility of intervention by China, the Indian Government had decided that a posture of offensive defence would be maintained in the west.

The task of the Pakistani army in the western theatre, according to Major General (retired) Fazal Muqeem Khan in his book '*Pakistan's Crisis in Leadership*', was to seize the initiative at the start of hostilities and to capture as much Indian territory as possible. This would have brought about intolerable pressure on the Indian Government to negotiate in terms favourable to Pakistan. However, such an eventuality had already been anticipated by Indian planners and contingency plans were worked out accordingly. India's western border with Pakistan is a long one and traverses varied tracts of terrain such as mountains, fertile plains, desert and marshlands. Western and Southern Command Headquarters based at Simla and Pune respectively controlled this border, with the latter conducting operations during war from an advance headquarters at Jodhpur. Therefore the policy of the Indian Army on the western front, as already stated, was basically defensive in nature, restricted to only limited offensive actions.

15 Punjab (Patiala) at Hussainiwala

15 Punjab (Patiala) moved to Ferozepore in 1969 from the Naushera sector of Jammu & Kashmir. Its operational area was Hussainiwala, an enclave near Ferozepur on the western bank of the Sutlej which extends over an area of approximately eight hectares. As already stated, the command soon devolved from Lieutenant Colonel J.S.

Indo-Pak War – 1971

Sandhu to G.B.V.L. Sastry. The latter was an officer of good professional standing and had been Mentioned-in-Despatches in the 1965 War while with 7 Punjab.

The unit lost no time in establishing itself at Ferozepur as the finest unit in the division. It made a mark in operational, training and sports activities and was on the pinnacle of success when the 1971 Indo-Pak War broke out. It fell to the lot of this gallant battalion to fight the famous battle of Hussainiwala.

The Hussainiwala enclave borders Pakistan, and the road connecting Ferozepur with Kasur and Lahore passed through the enclave. The international traffic was controlled by a joint Indo-Pakistan Checkpost, known as JCP in the local parlance. At the checkpost Pakistan had its Sutlej Rangers while India had elements of its Border Security Force. The two nations also had their customs and immigration department personnel at the checkpost. As on the Wagah Border, the Indo-Pak highway was ceremonially closed every evening at dusk and this ritual attracted a number of spectators from both sides of the border. Hussainiwala sector included the head-works and the landmass on the Pakistan side of the Sutlej upto the international border. The terrain is low lying and interspersed with numerous flood-cum-check bunds criss-crossing. These bunds forced linear deployment and provided no depth. At places, forward defended localities were only 300 yards from the international border.

Consequent to large scale mobilization on the eastern front, the battalion moved to Hussainiwala enclave to prevent the enemy from capturing the Hussainiwala headworks and bridge intact.

Of significance is the fact that the Hussainiwala salient affords protection to a considerable civil engineering structure comprising the head-works on the Sutlej with its elaborate sluice gates. It also provided the embankment over which ran the road and railway to Pakistan. The railway had not, however, been used since long. The sluice gates, controlling the release of water for irrigation on the Indian side, could only be operated from the enclave side of the head-works. The memorials to the famed martyrs of India's struggle for independence, namely, Bhagat Singh and Rajguru, which had the status of a national shrine, were located in the enclave. Militarily, the enclave provided a launch pad across the Sutlej for the advance of 7 Infantry Division to Kasur, as in 1965. The enclave was traversed by a number of flood control embankments called 'bunds' which provided excellent dominating positions for weapons. The areas between the bunds were low lying, prone to waterlogging, and in many places they were overgrown with *Sarkanda*' or tall grass, typical of such riverine tracts of the plain.

In October 1971 the responsibilities for the Hussainiwala-Ferozepur areas changed hands. 14 Infantry Division had then assumed control of Faridkot-Momdot-Fazilka area. Consequently, 35 Infantry Brigade commanded by Brigadier Pran Anand, VSM, took charge of the Ferozepur-Hussainiwala area with 15 Punjab allotted to him. Thus 15 Punjab of 29 Infantry Brigade was placed under 35 Infantry Brigade which in turn was removed from 14 Infantry Division and placed under control of 7 Infantry Division.

35 Infantry Brigade was deployed on the east of the Sutlej, leaving 15 Punjab on the west side of the river, within the enclave. The brigade headquarters was established in Ferozepur while the divisional headquarters was about seventy kilometres away in Patti. The battalion was now operating under a totally new brigade headquarters which,

in turn, was looking up to another new formation headquarters. The deployment of the other two battalions of 35 Infantry Brigade remained disassociated with that of 15 Punjab, which was operating independently in the enclave.

The operational deployment of the battalion within the enclave corresponded to the flood control bunds that covered the approaches to the head-works-cum-bridge area. The most vulnerable part of the defence, namely, the 'Perimeter' area, only a few yards from the border and looked into the Kikar post of Pakistan, was entrusted to 'D' company. Major Kanwaljit Singh, the company commander, was a popular and pragmatic officer. He was fearless in action and had only recently been awarded the Shaurya Chakra for saving the life of a soldier from the accidental burst of a grenade. The approach astride the main road, inclusive of the brick kiln tower in the 'Samadhi' area, was with 'C' company. It was expected that this locality would, in every eventuality, play an important role in the battle. Major S.P.S. Waraich, in command of this company, was a dedicated officer with a military family background. The northern flank of the battalion's defences were held by 'A' company on 'Kunde Bund' with one of its platoons extended to the area of 'Sand Dunes'. Its company commander was Major Hardyal Singh. In the battalion's linear pattern of defence, depth was provided by 'B' company on 'Guide Bund' under Major Narain Singh, a fine regimental officer who preferred to carry a rifle instead of the authorized carbine. That apart, a group of soldiers who had been recalled from the reserves alongwith elements of other rifle companies, had been formed into an ad hoc company and were located at 'Twin Canals', on the south eastern bank of the Sutlej.

The battalion, having been deployed mostly within the enclave, had its headquarters located outside the enclave in a cellar-like space below the canal bungalow, which housed the office and rest house of the Irrigation Department. The siting of the battalion headquarters, outside the very enclave which was to be defended, was an unfortunate tactical error. The decision was based on the premise that it would move to 'Guide Bund' in the enclave when hostilities were imminent. It was unfortunate but true that not one of the string of senior commanders who had visited the site over the years, or had war-gamed the defensive battle, had questioned the wisdom of the headquarters being located away from the enclave, with a major river flowing between the two. In a deployment where the battalion was sited virtually on the border, there could have been no warning of the attack when it came. This cost the battalion very dearly, for when the offensive did come it denied the effective leadership of the commanding officer, which is so essential in battle.

The area north of the battalion's defences had been entrusted to 25th Battalion of the Border Security Force. Its headquarters was at 'Finger', a narrow bund, where Captain Rawat was the liaison officer from 15 Punjab. As for armour, one troop of tanks of 3 Cavalry was available for use in battle. This was located nearer Ferozpore, on the premise that enough warning would be available. The artillery support was guaranteed by 5 Field Regiment and 223 Medium Regiment, while fire support was planned to be made available from other elements of the divisional artillery.

The plan of the enemy was to attack along Kasur-Ferozepur road with infantry and armour, and capture Hussainiwala bridge intact, if possible, by his coup-de-main, and thereafter to capture Ferozepore. The southern end of Hussainiwala bridge was reportedly planned to be captured by heliborne troops. This would have totally isolated the enclave. By the end of November, the move of Pakistani

106 Infantry Brigade to its battle locations had gone unnoticed by the Indian intelligence organizations, though its presence in the area of Kasur was a known fact. It is to the credit of Pakistani battalions that their move, quite close to the international border in the attack configuration, was fully concealed from the observation posts of 15 Punjab. The heavy traffic of men and vehicles from Pakistan continued across the JCP, and the stream of passengers entering India had no inkling of the goings on immediately on the other side of the border. In short, all appeared normal. The routine in defences went on as usual in the enclave, since the commanding officer had insisted on the standard operating procedures being strictly followed by the battalion.

On 3 December, Subedar Major Hardev Singh was to proceed on pension. Instead of the usual *'bara-khana'* and farewell functions which a battalion would normally accord to its elders going on pension, a severely curtailed regime was followed. The Subedar Major went round bidding farewell to each company locality during the day, and was joined by some officers and JCOs at a farewell tea party organised near the canal bungalow in the afternoon. The war broke out well after the Subedar Major had left for Ferozepore, only that this gallant JCO immediately returned to the battalion and remained with it till well after the war ended.

At about 6.35 p.m. on 3 December 1971, the enemy started intense and prolonged artillery shelling on the entire battalion defended area. It was later revealed that enemy's entire corps artillery was employed for Hussainiwala operation. This was followed by an attack employing four infantry battalions and a squadron of armour. The ambitious enemy plan, relying on surprise and overwhelming superiority of number and artillery, had visualized reaching the environs of Ferozepore two hours after the attack went in at last light. Against heaviest odds, while some ground was lost, a major portion of the Patiala company localities held out in spite of heavy attack. The enemy's efforts to smash through were blunted, to an extent where it could not even exploit its gains and seize the bridge intact.

A fierce battle continued throughout the night of 3/4 December 1971, with each company beating back determined enemy attacks in overwhelming strength several times. The enemy attacked Major Kanwaljit's Perimeter and Major Waraich's Samadhi localities simultaneously with 3 Punjab and 41 Baluch respectively, while its 19 Punjab was kept in reserve for the Pakistani brigade Phase II operations. 15 Punjab's 'D' and 'C' companies brought down a murderous volume of fire of automatic weapons from their locations. The enemy, nevertheless, achieved good success against the Samadhi area. This was due to 'C' company not having yet got into its 'Stand to' positions, in keeping with the existing orders, due to the Pakistani traffic having only just been cleared from the area.

Around daybreak on 4 December, a clearer picture emerged. While Perimeter and Samadhi areas were in enemy hands, the companies on Guide and Kunde Bunds had held their own. The positions were well stocked, and the defences had stood up well to the pounding by enemy artillery. Despite casualties, and a rather large number of men reported missing, the troops were in good spirit. In the confused aftermath of this gallant action the Samadhi Tower, or, 'Qajser Hind' as the Pakistanis' called it, changed hands twice before the enemy occupied its ground floor. On the upper portion of this tower Naik Surjit Singh, with his medium machine gun detachment and about a section of 'C' company, held the attackers at bay the attackers by sheer audacity and cold courage. All attempts by the enemy to rush the stairs were foiled by this dauntless group, till the early hours of the next day.

Naik Surjit Singh and his men on the Samadhi Tower's top had displayed cool gallantry, which had cheered every one up. Pakistani tanks had been brought up close to the tower to finally destroy the occupants above. A few tank shots blasted through the room, which seriously injured Naik Surjit Singh in the arm. Instead of giving up, as was expected by the enemy, the NCO and his detachment forced their way out of the tower with weapons blazing. Some were killed, some bayonetted, but the rest came out. None had surrendered. On that day the IAF claimed 20 Pakistani tanks and over 20 vehicles hit.

Major Waraich could not be contacted soon after the attack started. Eye-witnesses reported later that he and his men had beaten back a series of assaults till they were overwhelmed. Major Waraich could not be traced after this, although conflicting reports circulated that he had either fallen or had been taken prisoner. The latter seemed more plausible, since his body could not be traced thereafter. The enemy's attack had thus broken through 'C' company, and soon its leading troops were in contact with 'B' company at 'Guide Bund'.

'D' company at Perimeter proved to be a different proposition to the enemy. Major Kanwaljit had organised a tight defence, which had held the very courageous assault launched by the Pakistani 3 Punjab. The enemy then attacked again, and the loud conversation of the attacking forces indicated that the commanding officer of the enemy battalion was himself present on the scene. This attack was also beaten back after Pakistani troops had nearly reached the bridge on the river. This led to a near total break up of Pakistan's 3 Punjab, which had lost quite a few officers, including its commanding officer. In fact, at one stage, a Pakistani officer who was nearly succeeding in his bid to capture 'Perimeter' was left with no more than a handful of men.

The Samadhi defences having been also overwhelmed by the enemy, the latter soon attempted to rush its tanks on the bridge. On seeing an enemy tank move, Major Kanwaljit rushed out to lay a mine 'necklace' on the path of the tank, but was hit in the bargain. Regardless of his injuries, the officer took over the recoilless gun near the road and fired at the rushing enemy tank, which halted as a consequence of being hit.

From 3 a.m. onwards, enemy launched fresh attacks with infantry, to include a company of 19 Punjab alongwith an additional troop of armour, but these were repulsed by the remaining companies with the help of effective artillery fire. By 7 am on 4 December, the companies along the river line were holding out, though in a reduced area since their forward localities had fallen to the enemy.

At about 10.30 pm the bridge blew up due to a sympathetic detonation. Soon after this, an Indian tank of 7 Cavalry, which had gone across the bridge, came rushing back and, not knowing that the bridge had blown, fell headlong into the river. The crew of the fallen tank, who were dazed and shaken, never knew what happened. They would not have survived had it not been for the timely action taken by the Patialas. The crew was recovered during the night. In a daring action, Captain M.S. Sibia led the rescue patrol under heavy enemy fire, which proceeded to the river bed. Despite accurate fire opened up by the enemy from 'Perimeter' area, by now in enemy hands, Captain Sibia's men gallantly rescued and brought back the entire tank crew to safety.

Later in the day the enemy was seen preparing to launch fresh infantry – armour attacks against the remaining troops holding on. The tenacity of the Patialas and effective artillery and air strikes kept the enemy at bay. However, as soon as the aircraft went back, enemy infantry and armour would move up and attempt to nibble at the defence. This back and forth struggle went on throughout the day. By now the casualties had piled up with no possibility of evacuation, and the troops were running low on ammunition. No reinforcements on boats through the river were feasible due to effective enemy interference. There was also no room in the enclave to deploy any additional troops.

At this stage the unit received orders to withdraw. In contrast with a display of sheer grit and sacrifice, the orders to abandon the enclave came as a blow to one and all within it. It was difficult to believe the orders, but they were true. The officers had a difficult time explaining the rationale of withdrawal to the men. In keeping with the disciplined traditions, after the initial disbelief, the troops set about organising the withdrawal. The first requirement was to avoid giving an inkling to the enemy about the plans. This was achieved by regrouping the extended sub-units under cover of artillery shots, and some aggressive measures against enemy pockets that had emboldened to close in. The companies at Kunde and Guide Bunds closed ranks and presented as intact a front as they possibly could. As the cold December night fell, the troops fell back in pneumatic boats. The casualties were taken out first and as mid-night approached, the battalion was across the river. Surprise had been total, as the enemy noisily attacked Kunde and Guide Bunds at mid-night to find them vacant.

The thought of withdrawal had, in fact, never occurred to anyone in the battalion which had brought to a halt a brigade attack supported by a divisional artillery and armour.

The battalion lost two officers and 53 other ranks were killed. Three JCOs and 31 other ranks were also wounded. In addition, two JCOs and 35 other rank were repatriated after the cease-fire. The proven gallantry of its officers like Major Kanwaljit Singh and Major Wariach, and scores of its brave men who had grimly fought the Pakistanis and brought their attack to a halt, bears testimony to the valour and dogged determination of the Patialas. The reputation of the battalion was upheld when, after the Simla Accord, the Pakistanis returning the Hussainiwala enclave paid unstinted praise to its valour and sacrifices. This was soon followed by the publication of the book *Pakistan's Crisis in Leadership* by Major General (retired) Fazal Muqueem Khan which acknowledged the gallantry of the battalion in unequivocal terms. He has stated in his book :- "The Indian 15 Punjab fought extremely well, although they had been abandoned by its neighbouring troops. They were fully supported by extensive artillery fire from the other side of the river." It is a unique privilege of the battalion to have been honoured by the opponents in battle.

The battalion was awarded the Theatre Honour 'Punjab – 71' in recognition of its services at Hussainiwala.

11

The Post – 1971 War Era

After the battle of Hussainiwala the unit reverted to its parent formation, 29 Infantry Brigade, and, on 6 December 1971 occupied positions on the Ditch-cum-Bund in the Khem Karan area where it remained till 1973. During March 1972 Lieutenant Colonel V.R. Raghavan (later Lieutenant General and Colonel of the Punjab Regiment, now retired), assumed command.

After returning from the Khem Karan sector the battalion stayed at its permanent location at Ferozepore for a brief period of two months. Thereafter it moved to its next field location at Charmaged, on the Indo-Tibetan border, in June 1973, where it was placed under 69 Mountain Brigade. During its stint here the unit carried out extensive training, and its performance in various competitions and innumerable operational tasks, were of an exceptionally high order, earning considerable praise.

Lieutenant Colonel Rajinder Singh assumed command of the battalion on 20 July 1975. Under his tenure the unit moved to Gwalior where it formed part of 72 Infantry Brigade from September 1976 to December 1980. As usual the Patialas left an indelible imprint in this formation also, and went on to win many more laurels. Lieutenant Colonel

B.S. Grewal took over the command of the Patialas on 9 June 1979.

From Gwalior the battalion moved to Tenga Valley where it came under the orbat of 5 Mountain Division. In May 1981 Lieutenant Colonel (later Major General, now retired) Shivdev Singh assumed command. The long stint at Tenga and Bhuri, totalling more than three and a half years, was a challenging chapter in the unit's history. Having seen three different operational areas, the unit was also involved for one year in the construction of defences at high altitudes. It also had the proud privilege of receiving a number of VIP visitors, to include the Chief of Army Staff.

Lieutenant Colonel H.S. Brar assumed command of the battalion on 3 August 1983, while the battalion was still at Tenga Valley. After the hard tenure in the east, the Patialas arrived at Meerut on 16 April 1984. Hardly had they settled down when the situation in Punjab began to deteriorate considerably, and soon enough the call came for the Patialas to move to Punjab to participate in 'Op Blue Star'. It operated in the Hoshiarpur district from May to September 1984 and again from November 1984 to February 1985.

This was possibly the toughest test for this battle scarred unit, which had a glorious history of nearly three centuries. When a number of other battle scarred and seasoned Sikh units fell apart, the Patialas proved to be a shining example of outstanding discipline and steadfastness to their country, leaders and the Regiment. Not only did they maintain a high standard of loyalty and integrity throughout the turbulent period, they also executed all sensitive operational tasks in a most exemplary manner. The Patialas earned praise of both the locals and commanders up the chain for tactful handling of the volatile situation.

The Post – 1971 War Era

The unit earned a good name in matters of training too, and was always specially earmarked for organizing important demonstrations and presentations on professional subjects. Headquarters 32 Infantry Brigade was so impressed with the training and high standard of the Patialas that almost all VIPs were brought to the unit to see its performance in these fields. On 1 March 1986 Colonel S Hoon took over the reins and went on to command the battalion for one and a half years.

After Meerut the unit again moved to Ladakh, this time to Kaksar in the Dras sector. Unlike the epic battle of Zojila fought in 1948 in the frozen heights of Zojila Pass, which has been well illustrated in this book and is now part and parcel of the Patiala folklore, its next major operation fought in Dalunang, are chronicled in the following chapter.

12

Battle of Dalunang

Forty years after the heroic battle of Zojila, 15 Punjab (Patiala) fought another important battle at Dalunang in the Ladakh region, an innocuous place near Dras on the Dras-Kaksar-Leh highway, about 70 kilometres north of the Zojila Pass. The exemplary courage, devotion to duty and the fighting skills exhibited by the unit in this encounter with the enemy bear testimony to the valour and bravery of the Patialas in a new, modern era.

Dalunang is a small sleepy village, or a group of small hamlets located on the Indian side of the Line of Control (LC), overlooking the bank of the Kaksar river. It is flanked by high mountain ridges on all sides. Its strategic value lies in its being in the infiltration route to Kaksar, near Kargil, which, if captured, could cut off the Dras-Kaksar-Kargil highway – the lifeline of Leh and Ladakh.

Over a period of years the enemy had slowly but surely sent in troops surreptitiously and taken possession of this group of small hamlets, claiming it to be a part of their territory. The Pakistani battalion deployed in the region at that time was 3 Northern Light Infantry (NLI), which was commanded by Lieutenant Colonel Ahmed Chatha. This battalion formed part of Pakistan's 80 Infantry Brigade which

Battle of Dalunang

was commanded by Brigadier Mohmmad Aziz Khan from his Headquarters based at Minimarg. The Patiala's, after being inducted into the 121 (Independent) Infantry Brigade sector which was commanded by Brigadier MS Puri, detected the occupation through a patrol sent to the area.

On discovery of this intrusion, a series of flag meetings at the battalion and brigade level were held, but the Pakistanis continued to claim Dalunang to be their territory. They gave some ambiguous reasons to justify their occupation of Dalunang, which were strongly contested by the Indian Commanders. As no headway could be made on this sensitive issue, the Indians decided to restore status quo ante. Soon the Patialas were given the responsibility of evicting the encroachment, if need be by using force, a task taken up by the battalion with enthusiasm and alacrity. It involved removing the well entrenched enemy from dominating heights along the ridge lines, a test of supreme human endurance against the heaviest of odds.

The unit, which was actively involved in operations in this area from 22 August 1988 to 22 May 1989, sent out numerous other patrols to assess enemy deployment and its lines of communication. As a result it became evident that Pakistani troops had made surreptitious inroads into certain areas and occupied heights well within Indian territory, which not only overlooked Dalunang village but also dominated the national highway linking Srinagar to Leh at Kaksar, by observation and fire. The Patialas soon took possession of certain unoccupied neighbouring posts and also brought forth heavy and effective fire against the enemy posts. In the process the Patialas were able to not only dominate certain posts illegally occupied by the Pakistanis, but were also able to block their lines of communications, including a nearby water point which the Pakistani were depending upon. In a bid to counter the Patialas, the enemy also managed to severe the supply route of one of the companies of 15 Punjab (Patiala). As a result, this company was left with no food or water for a number of days. However, this deprivation only made the Patiala soldiers mentally stronger, and they continued to stick to their task with sincerity of purpose.

In the ensuing months the firing continued and the onset of winters did not see any decline in the intensity of firing. After the melting of snow during the spring of 1989, the Patialas, under the cover of heavy mortar, automatic weapons and artillery fire, rushed towards the enemy posts in broad daylight. The enemy, sitting in prepared positions, was taken aback by total surprise, sheer ferocity and momentum of attack. Even though it retaliated with automatic and mortar fire, due to the sheer weight of the Patiala attack Pakistani troops were pushed back from a number of locations, and Patiala soldiers occupied these posts and simultaneously established six new posts right under the nose of the enemy.

Thereafter, sporadic battles continued over the next few months. Despite being under tremendous pressure due to its own administrative tail having been repeatedly cut off by the enemy, the Patialas never flinched their responsibilities and stuck to their task with vigour. The enemy, which met with a series of reverses, tried its level best to re-capture lost posts and establish some additional posts, but the determined Patialas remained forever alert and foiled all such attempts of the enemy.

The Patiala's commanding officer, Lieutenant Colonel MS Sibia, personally ensured the defence of own posts against repeated enemy attacks, and throughout continued to inspire his troops by his towering leadership. One of the threatened posts held by the Patialas was commanded by Major RR Nimbhorkar. Inspite of enemy pressure he rallied his men

Battle of Dalunang

from the brink and bunched them together as a cohesive team. As a result, repeated assaults onto his post by the enemy proved futile. Captain A. Saini, too, kept his calm throughout this crucial period and provided inspiring leadership to the men under his command at a critical juncture.

The prompt offensive action taken by the unit resulted in the enemy's overall demoralization and subsequent dissipation of retaliatory response, resulting in his final withdrawal from Dalunang.

The Patialas suffered nine fatal casualties (including three JCOs) and 22 wounded. It stands to the credit of the wounded that they volunteered to be recycled back despite their physical handicaps. Conversely, enemy suffered 19 casualties and 49 wounded, out of which many died during evacuation subsequently, thereby forcing Pakistan to open a new Military Hospital (MH) at Skardu.

What is noteworthy is that the Pakistani commanding officer, Lieutenant Colonel Ahmed Chatha, frequently requested the Patialas for cease-fire during the operations so as to enable him to extricate his wounded and dead. While withdrawing, Pakistan had to vacate illegally occupied villages of Babachand and Silyar totally and Thanus partially. This created problems of refugee resettlement and rehabilitation of locals for the enemy.

The saga of Dalunang speaks volumes of Pakistan's nefarious designs and Indian Army's tenacity and dogged determination, particularly of 1st Patiala which had earlier operated with distinction in the high altitude and inhospitable terrain of nearby Zojila 40 years ago. The high mountains of Dalunang bear mute testimony to the gallant battles fought by the brave soldiers of this unit, which helped the Indians in retaining the sanctity of the strategically important Kaksar and also of the Drass-Kaksar-Kargil-Leh highway.

For its gallant effort and devotion to duty the unit was bestowed with a number of honours and awards, to include one Yudh Seva Medal (YSM), two Sena Medals (SM), one Mentioned-in-Despatches, three COAS's Commendation Cards and five GOC's Commendation Cards. Amongst the awardees were the commanding officer who was awarded the YSM, and Majors (now Colonels) RR Nimbhorkar and SS Sihag, who received Sena Medals respectively.

Within five years the Patialas went on to earn many more laurels in the state of Jammu & Kashmir, albeit in the highly intricate and specialized field of counter-insurgency operations in the Valley. But before that the unit went on to excel in other stations such as Dras and Miran Sahib, under the command of M.S. Sibia, and M.S. Kalra respectively.

13

Towards Countering the Proxy War

"Campaigns of this kind are more likely to continue, because it is the only kind of war that fits the conditions of the modern age, while being at the same time well suited to take advantage of social discontent, racial ferment and national fervours."

—Liddell Hart (1962)

Kashmir—A Volatile State

The Kashmir problem, which exists ever since India gained independence and the state ceded to India following Pakistan's bid to annex it, has led to three major wars between the two countries. Though the causes leading to all the wars have already been covered in the respective chapters, suffice to say that Pakistan has annexed more than two thirds of Jammu and Kashmir as a result of its invasion in 1947-48. With the dismemberment of Pakistan and more than 90,000 Pakistani troops taken captive by Indian troops following their surrender in erstwhile East Pakistan as a result of the 1971 Indo-Pak War, a deep scar was left in the psyche of the military leaders of Pakistan. They have always wanted to redeem their humiliation and endeavoured to exploit every ethnic problem that India faced, like the Punjab and Kashmir problems, to name a few. The on-going Kashmir imbroglio is perhaps the most complex of India's problems, to be exploited by Pakistan by way of a remote controlled 'Proxy War'. Four rounds of military conflicts, a decade long proxy war, numerous negotiations, track two initiatives, attempts at back channel diplomacy, agreements and summits notwithstanding, a solution continues to defy India. The situation today has assumed grave dimensions, as the socio-political landscape of the Valley lies fractured and embittered, belying the age-old description of Kashmir as 'a paradise on earth'.

The army was roped in to tackle the deteriorating situation in the State right from the beginning, when the so called 'law and order' problems became difficult for the state administration to handle. Thereafter the army had to manage its affairs on two fronts, that of border guarding and internal security duties. The latter included conducting counter-infiltration and counter-terrorist operations as well. Army posts, particularly along the Line of Control, are mainly located on hilly and ruggedly mountainous terrain, often covered by dense snow during winters. At many such posts there prevails eyeball to eyeball confrontation between troops of the two armies. Numerous gaps existing all along the border enable many groups of terrorists to cross over into Indian territory to create mayhem.

Militancy picked up tempo in the state of Jammu and Kashmir in the nineties because Pakistan's focus, which was all this while on the war in neighbouring Afghanistan, shifted to this state. Pakistan provided all the support to various terrorist groups by way of finance, weapons and the establishment of various training bases and camps all along the Line of Control.

In numerous brigades or sectors of Jammu and Kashmir various battalions of the Indian army have repeatedly held

Towards Countering the Proxy War 179

picquets face to face with Pakistani troops. Incidences of enhanced firing and border provocation of various kinds, particularly during infiltration, are frequent in such areas, often causing casualties. Retaliation of such provocation, at times, involves physical and tactical efforts, often in adverse terrain and weather conditions. However, before going any further it will be pertinent to briefly describe the distinct regions of the state and also the various sectors deployed along the border.

As already covered briefly, the state of Jammu & Kashmir as it exists today can be divided into three distinct regions, viz the Ladakh region towards the northeast of the state, the Kashmir region in the north and the Jammu region in the south. Whereas the first two are physically divided by the formidable, snow capped Great Himalayan Range running northwest to southeast, the Jammu region is divided by the forested Pir Panjal Range running east to west. The entire hinterland north of Pir Panjal range, less the formidable forested (and densely snow covered during winters) Shamsabari range further up north, and Ladakh toward the east, is very fertile and is commonly referred to as the 'Valley'. South of Pir Panjal Range, in the districts of Doda-Udhampur-Rajouri-Poonch, the terrain is mountainous, treacherous and covered with dense forests providing safe havens for floating terrorist groups. In the plains sector of Jammu region, roughly between Jammu and Pathankot, lies the International border, although Pakistan mischievously refers to it as the 'working boundary' since it considers the entire state of Jammu and Kashmir as disputed territory. In this particular stretch, the border guarding is being done by the BSF, although quite a few military cantonments are also located relatively close to the border.

Further towards the west of Jammu is the sector comprising of the plains of Akhnoor and Jaurian and a portion of the Sunderbani, or the Kalidhar hill tracts. Further up north, in the Indian 25 Infantry Divisional sector, the terrain comprises hills varying in height from 700 to more than 4000 metres. While low lying sector, culminating into the western reaches of the Pir Panjal ranges.

North of the Pir Panjal Range, along the Shamshabari Range there are posts located at heights, many above 3,000 metres, which remain snow bound throughout the winter months. Further to the east, beyond the Zojila Pass is the high altitude Ladakh sector. Where the terrain is rugged, mountainous and barren, and remains snow bound most of the year. The Kargil war, codenamed 'Op Vijay', was fought in this sector during mid 1999. The famous Siachen Glacier, shaped like a dagger, pointing Northwards lies in this region. Indian troops deployed in this sector are operating under the charter of 'Op Meghdoot'.

Demographically, the Ladakh sector has a sparse Buddhist majority population, where Buddhists comprise 78% of the population. The remaining comprises 18% Shia Muslim population in the Kargil sector. The remaining 4% comprise Hindus and other religions. The entire Valley comprises a dense Sunni Muslim majority population. Similarly, south of the Pir Panjal ranges a Muslim majority population exists in the districts of Poonch, Rajouri, northern half of Udhampur and Doda. However, in the remaining districts of Udhampur and Doda and the entire area further south towards the foothills and the plains, the population is mainly Hindu. Noteworthy is the fact that the percentage of Muslims in the valley is more than double of all the Muslims in the other two regions of Ladakh and Jammu.

Towards Countering the Proxy War

Thus, the 1990s saw a spurt of Pak sponsored terrorist activities in the state based on local and foreign mercenaries to include Pakistani and Afghani nationals, all funded and trained at various bases and training camps located at many places in Pakistan and POK, close to the international border and the Line of Control respectively. As a result of this 'Proxy' or remote controlled war against India in the state its borders were kept alive through frequent firing of automatic weapons missiles and artillery so as to facilitate smooth infiltration and ex-filtration of various terrorist groups.

The sharp rise in the fundamentalist thrust of the secessionist movement, with a distinct communal undertones, caused panic among the non-Muslims in the valley and hastened the pace of migration which acquired the form of mass exodus by the end of February 1990. Around 30,000 families of Hindus and 2,000 of Sikhs migrated from the valley to safer places in Jammu and other places in the country till end March 1990.

Based on the terrain and demographic profile, it will emerge that terrorist groups prefer to infiltrate to and fro the valley along the rugged, forest covered mountain ranges and mingle with the locals in the Muslim majority areas for avoiding detection. After receiving training in various training camps located in Pakistan and POK, the various militant groups, infiltrate into the state with the help of local guides. They establish bases in remote areas where the terrain is difficult and the population Muslim, but sparse. These terrorist bases, which are invariably well stocked with rations, arms, ammunition and subversive material, would shift to the upper reaches during summers and come down to below the snowline during winters.

In order to contain enemy action and sponsored terrorism in the volatile state, various battalions of the

Punjab Regiment, particularly 15 Punjab (Patiala), have come out with flying colours in conducting successful operations under the banner of 'Op Rakshak'.

The Taming of Baramula

15 Punjab (Patiala) was inducted into the Baramula Sector, where it formed part of 79 Mountain Brigade, on 18 June 1992. It was assigned the operational role along the Line of Control and also conducted offensive counter insurgency operations in the depth areas. Under the command of Colonel K.S. Aithmian the unit's performance was outstanding indeed. It had the rare distinction of bringing normalcy to the volatile urban centre of Baramula, with a population of about 55,000, within a period of just three months.

During May 1994 the unit moved to Watergam to subdue insurgents of the notorious Rafiabad belt. The unit was successful to neutralise most of the terrorists in that area, where it had eliminated 23 and apprehended 37 terrorists apart from recovering 43 weapons of various types. The Patialas developed a unique style of conducting specialized counter-terrorist operations. Not only did they establish their own, extremely reliable intelligence network, but they also had an uncanny knack of moving around their area of responsibility in small groups dressed and armed like local terrorists. They were able to move from one flashpoint to another with alacrity, and their modus operandi was so effective that not only did they win the trust of the locals of the area, but many of them, to include the aged men, women and children also volunteered to assist the Patialas in various ways, while many others offered their services as guides, spotters and interlocutors between various militant groups and belligerent individuals.

Towards Countering the Proxy War

Till 31 March 1995 the battalion had recovered 396 weapons of all types, eliminated 102 terrorists of various cadres, or 'Tanzeems', and apprehended another 447 terrorists. The unit was deinducted on 10 April 1995 for its subsequent move to Kanpur.

While in the valley the unit lived upto its glorious traditions. Due to its excellent performance, the brave Patialas earned one Kirti Chakra, which was awarded to Sepoy Gurtej Singh posthumously, two Shaurya Chakras, eleven Sena Medals (including one to the Commanding Officer), 14 COAS's Commendation Cards, 21 GOC-in-C's Commendation Cards, the coveted COAS's Unit Citation and the GOC-in-C's Unit Appreciation.

Sunderbani / Rajouri and Thereafter

But this was not the end of the saga of 1st Patiala in this state. Three years later, after a professionally most useful stint in Kanpur where the Patialas formed part of 62 Infantry Brigade of 4 Infantry Division, which came under the 1 (Strike) Corps, the battalion was again inducted into the state of Jammu & Kashmir. It moved under the command of Colonel Anil Shorey on 20 June 1998, this time to the Sunderbani Sector of 10 Infantry Division. It took over the defences of the Mala sub sector from 2 Maratha Light Infantry. This area is on the upper reaches of the Kalidhar ranges along the Line of Control. It had a company plus deployed on the Line of Control in the Mala sub-sector while the rest of the battalion was deployed in the counter insurgency grid in the hinterland, occupying an exceptionally large area of responsibility extending from Sunderbani to as far north as the Pir Panjal Range between Rajouri and Mohr tehsil of Udhampur district. Colonel R.R. Nimbhorkar, SM, took over the reigns of the battalion on 20 August 1998 from Colonel Shorey who proceeded to the Counter Insurgency Force 'Delta' as Colonel General Staff.

The 'Patialas' operated in this vast hinterland with elan and professionalism. It was able to neutralise a number of terrorists and recover a large amount of warlike stores. Between 11 to 16 June 1999 many special operations were launched by the veteran 'Patialas', causing heavy attrition on the enemy. Some of the operations conducted by Major D Choudhary, Captain Tejvir Singh, Captain V Bhardwaj, Captain N Bakshi and Subedar Jagir Singh alongwith the unit's 'Ghatak' platoon deserve special mention. In a particular incident two militants were killed by the battalion on 25 August 1999 while they were trying to infiltrate into India through the Mahadev gap. Naib Subedar Harmit Singh and his party were able to immediately react, which paid handsome dividends. However, when the Kargil War broke out in mid 1999, code named 'Operation Vijay' (Op Vijay), the entire battalion was concentrated along the Line of Control in the Mala sector in anticipation of enhanced infiltration attempts across the Line of Control, in consonance of Pakistan's game plan, where it achieved many successes.

From the very outset the battalion aggressively dominated the Line of Control in its area of responsibility, thereby lowering the enemy's morale and simultaneously achieving moral ascendancy over him throughout. That apart, a number of stand off attacks of the enemy were not only effectively repulsed but, as a result of the unit's proactive stance, the enemy suffered heavy casualties and a numbers of his bunkers were destroyed beyond recognition.

On 17 February 2000, during an operation led by Major D. Choudhary, the battalion team was able to kill two foreign terrorists in the area of Padri Gala. It conducted

Towards Countering the Proxy War

many other successful operations in the hinterland. Similarly, on 17 July 2000, two more terrorists were killed by Lance Naik Avtar Singh and Sepoy Dharmender Singh of the battalion while trying to infiltrate into India.

The finest hour of this battalion in this sector was when it eliminated eight foreign terrorists including one Turkish commander on 26 July 2000. This happened at the Ikhni Nala, which is a famous infiltration route in the 28 Infantry Brigade sector. This operation was masterminded by the second in command, Major D. Choudhary, who was assisted by Major Jaswinder Singh, Major J.S. Shekhawat, Subedars Karnail Singh and Balkar Singh. Apart from troops of 15 Punjab (Patiala), elements of 3 Grenadiers and 1812 Light Regiment also played a major role in eliminating the intruders.

Between December 1998 to end December 2000 the unit conducted ten very successful operations and eliminated a total of 24 hardcore terrorists, apart from recovering a large amount of arms, ammunitions, cash and other war like stores. This was the best record to have been established in the 10 Divisional Sector. On June 2001 Colonel Nimbhorkar relinquished command and proceeded to attend the coveted Higher Command Course, handing over command to Lieutenant Colonel Dipendra Sarin.

During this tenure the battalion earned one Sena Medal, three COAS's Commendation Cards and eight GOC-in-C's Commendation Cards. All these were earned without incurring a single fatal casualty. The 'Patialas' thereafter moved out for a well deserved peace tenure at Sri Ganganagar, where it was orbated to a formation of 16 Infantry Division.

FROM THE ARCHIVES

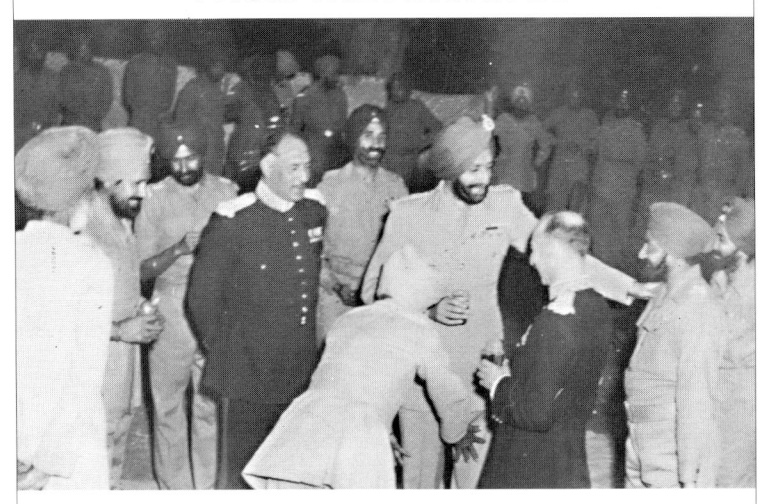

His Highness Yadvinder Singh during a visit to the unit's JCOs Mess with General KS Thimayya and LT Gen Hendrason Brooks - Gabdaan

Brigadier Dalip Singh, MBE, inspecting enemy 3:7" Howitzer captured during Zojila Operation. Also seen in picture are Lieutenant Colonel Bikram Dev Singh, DSO, Major Harchand Singh (retired) and Lieutenant Colonel Sukhdev Singh, MC, VrC - November 1950

The unit's hockey team, the proud winners
of PEPSU Championship Trophy - 19 December 1950

Group photo of ex CO's *(Left to Right)*. Lt Gen Balwant Singh
Sidhu, Col GS Sibia, Col JS Mandher, Brig HS Kullar,
Lt Col CS Dosanj and Lt Col JS Sandhu

Defence Minster Dr. KN Katju with Lieutenant General Kulwant Singh, Major General Bikram Singh and Brigadier SJ Thapa during their visit to 1st Patiala - 22 April 1956

His Highness visits 1st Patiala in Jammu & Kashmir in July 1962. Alongside him is Lt Col JS Mandher

Officers of 1st Patiala (Rajindra Sikh) in Mess Dress-1964.
Sitting from left - Lieutenant Subhash Chander, Lieutenant BN Chaturvedi, Major Inder Singh, Lieutenant Colonel HS Kullar, Major Inderjit Singh, Lieutenant PC Sood and Lieutenant RS Rajput.
Standing from left- Captains Ramesh Chhokra, ...*, Krishan Tule, SN Mishra, RB Bahie (RMO) and RB Parthartha
(*name not available)

Lt Gen PS Bhagat, VC, visiting the unit at Ferozpur - July 1970. Standing (extreme left) is CO, Lt Col GBVL Sastry

IN MEMORIAM

Paying tribute to the gallant Hussainiwala Martyrs

Colonel Shivdev Singh (later Maj Gen, now retd.) paying homage to deceased soldiers of the unit in NEFA

The war ravaged stationed towers in Hussainiwala

AT DRAS - J&K

Brigadier MS Puri, Commander 121(I) Infantry Brigade Group, Colonel MS Sibia, CO, Major General VR Raghavan, GOC 28 Infantry Division (a former unit CO and Col of the Regt) and Subedar Major Tehal Singh during the general officer's visit to the unit at Kaksar

His Holiness the Dalai Lama during his visit to the unit at Dras on 12 July 1988

Commanding Officer, Colonel Sibia with Lieutenant Colonel Ahmed Chatha, CO 3 NLI, during a flag meeting at Dalunang on 23 November 1988

General Joshi, COAS, during his visit to the unit at Baramula

DALUNANG MEMORIAL

INTRUSION DALUNANG
22 AUG 88 – 22 MAY 89

WE WILL REMEMBER THEM

IN THE EVERLASTING MEMORY OF THOSE GALLANT AND BRAVE SOLDIERS OF 15 PUNJAB (FIRST PATIALA RAJINDRA SIKH) WHO LAID DOWN THEIR LIVES AND DONE THE NATION PROUD BY FULFILLING THEIR TASK WITH EXTREME SELF SACRIFICE IN THE INTRUSION DALUNANG FROM 22 AUG 1988 – 22 MAY 1989.

INTRUSION DALUNANG IS AN EXAMPLE OF COURAGE MILITARY LEADERSHIP, TACTICAL ACUMEN EXTREME TENACITY AND SHEER HUMAN ENDURANCE IN THE WORST OF HARDSHIPS THAT THE BRAVE PANJABIS DISPLAYED FOR A PERIOD OF 9 MONTHS IN THE EXTREME DIFFICULT CLIMATIC CONDITIONS.

NATION WILL ALWAYS REMAIN PROUD OF THE FOLLOWING WHO SACRIFICED THEIR LIVES FOR THE MOTHER LAND.

Rank	Name	
Nb/SUB	SATNAM	SINGH
Nb/SUB	GURSEWAK	SINGH
Nb/SUB	MEHAR	SINGH
HAV	HARBANS	SINGH
NK	MUKHTIAR	SINGH
L/NK	DILBAGH	SINGH
L/NK	JAGTAR	SINGH
SEP	KABAL	SINGH
SEP	BUTA	SINGH

A view from Dalunang during winter - 1989

EXCELLING IN COUNTER-INSURGENCY ROLE- J&K

(Photos by Col Anil Shorey)

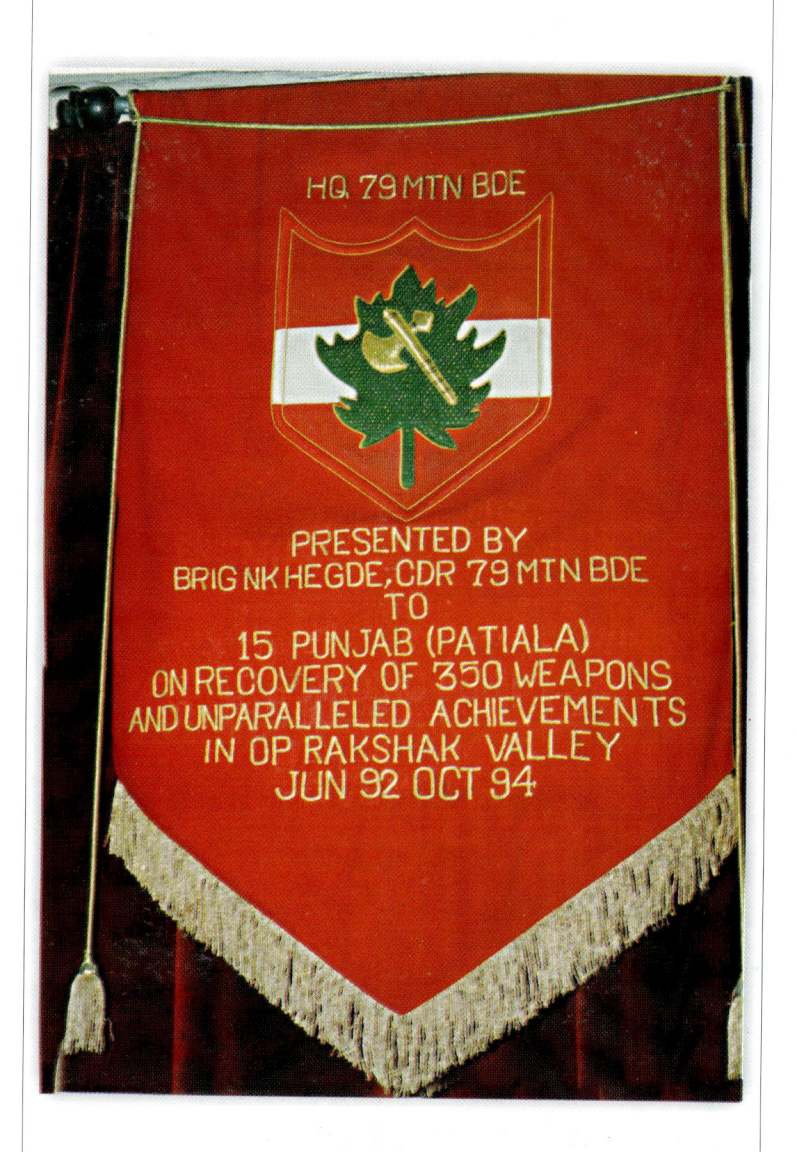

The 79 Mountain Brigade Banner

सेनाध्यक्ष से प्रशंसा

15 पंजाब ने जम्मू और कश्मीर के इलाके में नवम्बर 92 से जुलाई 93 तक सेवा करते हुए निम्नलिखित कार्य में अतिउत्तम सेवा, कर्तव्य निष्ठा, कार्य दक्षता एवं बहादुरी का परिचय दिया।

जम्मू और कश्मीर के बारामूला जिले में "आपरेशन रक्षक" के दौरान

इस कार्य के लिए मैं आपकी यूनिट की प्रशंसा करता हूँ।

नई दिल्ली

जनरल
सेनाध्यक्ष

COAS' Unit Citation

UNIT APPRECIATION BY GENERAL OFFICER COMMANDING-IN-CHIEF NORTHERN COMMAND

1. _15th Battalion The Panjab Regiment_ during its employment in Low Intensity Conflict Operations in the _Baramula District_ of Jammu and Kashmir from _June 92_ to _April 95_ has performed commendably.

2. The perseverance, devotion to duty and grit displayed by all ranks in dealing with the militants has been of a high order.

3. I congratulate all ranks of the unit for their excellent performance.

(Surinder Singh)
Lieutenant General
General Officer Commanding-in-Chief

GOC - in C's Unit Appreciation

HUSSAINIWALA - 1971

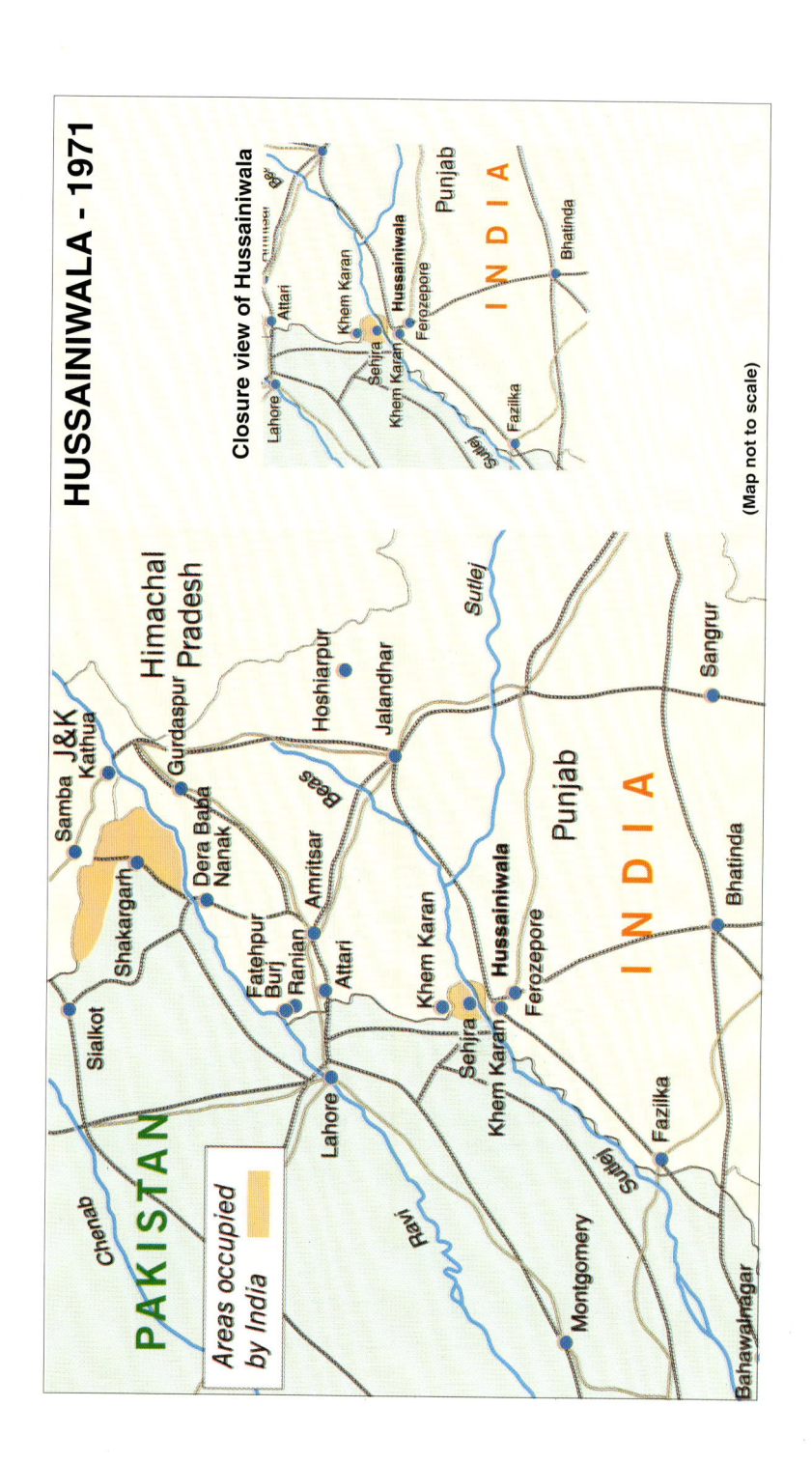

Closure view of Hussainiwala

(Map not to scale)

Areas occupied by India

DALUNANG, IN RELATION TO ZOJILA-DRAS-KARGIL

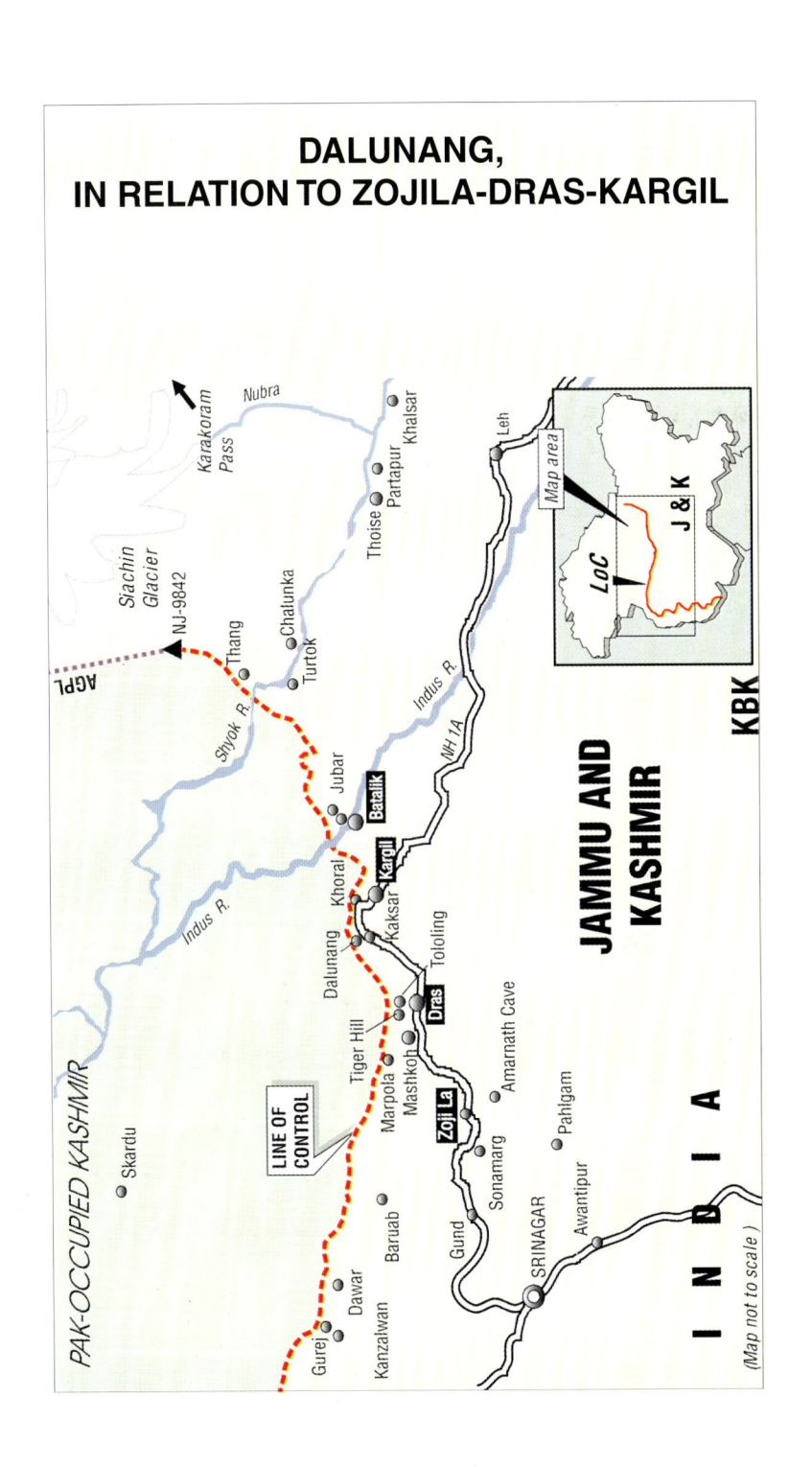

THE VALLEY AND JAMMU REGION - 1992-98

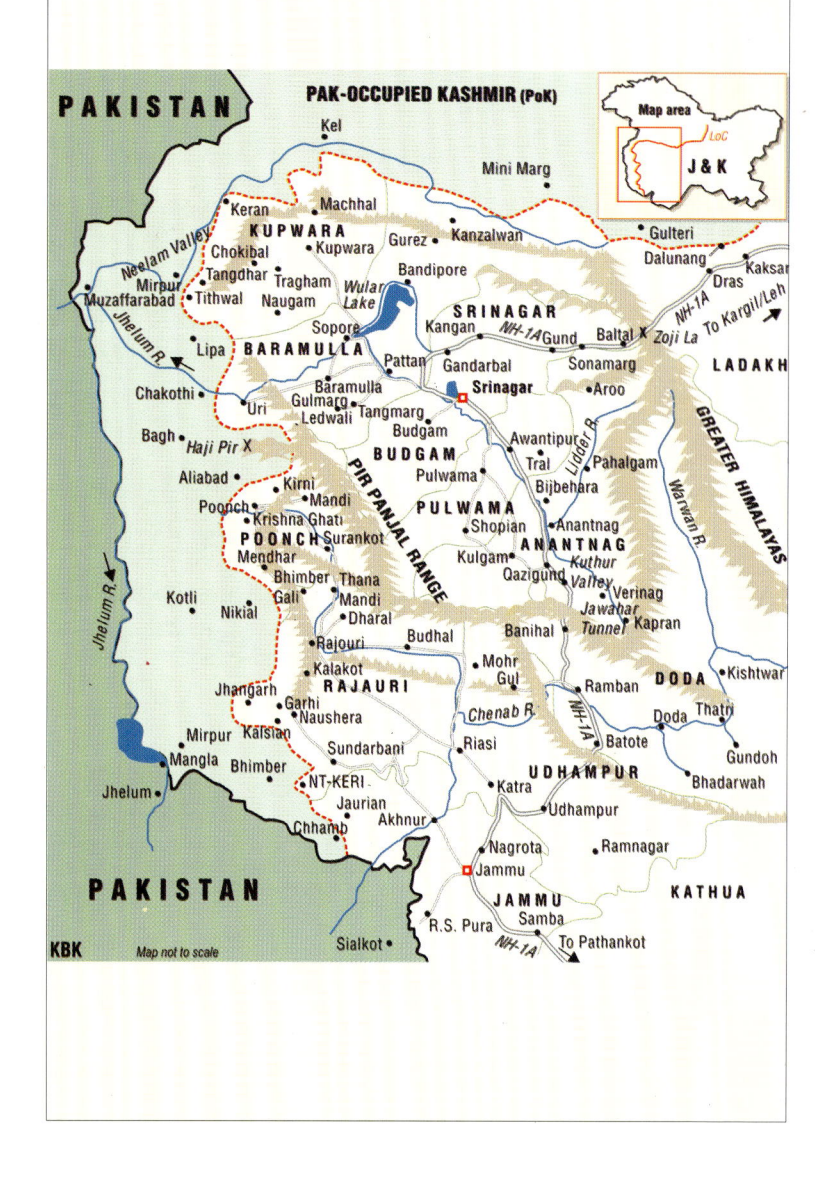

14

In the Western Sector

No sooner had the battalion settled down in its new location, a mass mobilization was ordered on 17 December 2001 as a result of 'Op Parakram'. The commanding officer, alongwith Captain Mohinder Lal and Lieutenant Vikas Sharma, who were holding the appointments of quartermaster and adjutant respectively, finilised and executed the unit's move schedule, and by 20 December the entire battalion was ready to be launched for any offensive task from its operational area in Karanpur sector. Preparation of defences was carried out simultaneously. Quality anti- tank ditches and an underground 'Ops Room' was constructed, and different minefields were also laid. The standard achieved by the unit in all these construction activities came in for a lot of praise by higer formations. The 'Ops Room', in particular, was so impressive that other units of the division were directed to construct their own respective 'Ops Rooms' on similar lines.

During the period spent in the operational area, training was given top priority by the unit. Battle drills and battle procedures, encompassing a wide array of operations of war, were rehearsed and fine - tuned to perfection. The

In the Western Sector

unit also drew the attention of a number of senior dignitaries, and amongst those who visited the battalion were Mr George Fernandes, the Defence Minister; Lieutenant Generals SS Mehta and BS Thakkar, Army Commander and Corps Commander respectievely. In December 2002 deinduction was ordered, and the unit reverted to its permanent location leaving a small rear party and the demining team behind. The task of demining the minefield was undertaken in a most efficient manner by Major Jaswinder Singh and Lieutenant Dinesh. The Patialas completed their task in record time, without incurring any casualty or injury. It was most creditable indeed.

The unit organised a spectacular display of weapons and equipment for the local population of Sri Ganganagar, particularly school children. The latter were so impressed that a vast majority took a pledge to opt for the army as a career, and the Patialas were bombarded with a plethora of queries related to army recruitment / commission. None went home disappointed; on the contrary, they all went home fully enthused and motivated, and before the unit completed its tenure, reports trickled in that seven of the local youth had joined the army; with three of them in the Punjab Regiment! In the field of sports and professional competitions, too, the Patialas bagged a number of trophies like the formation Basketball and Hockey Championship Trophy. In the Divisional Athletics, Lance Havildar Chanan Singh bagged the first prize in the Marathon. Amongst the other toppers were Sepoy Rajpal Singh in the 5 km and 1500 m run; Sepoy Balwinder stood in the 16 km run while Sepoy Daljit singh came first in the 10 km run and in 3000 m steple chase respectively.

On completion of its tenure at Sri Ganganagar, the unit moved to Gobindharh near Abohar, in the Fazilka Sector, in May 2004. It is a modified field area. On 18 June that year Colonel Advitya Madan assumed command of the unit, and his dual focus thereafter was concentrated on operationally oriented training and on planning for the conduct of the battalion's tricentenary scheduled on 13 April 2005 – Baisakhi Day. Apart from sprucing up the overall get up of the unit area, the blueprint for a motorcycle expedition to the mountainous town of Kaji in Himachal Pradesh was chalked out to coincide with the tricentenary- or tercentenary. A new tercentenary silver trophy was also conceived by the battalion, apart from lobbying for the release of a special postage stamp and the release of the battalion history book titled 'A Legendary Force – 1st Patiala' on the historic day. Incidentally the trophy has a unique design. Atop the three edges of its base, three silver Patiala soldiers stand guard majestically. A globe is placed atop a central silver pillar, highlighting various places where the battalion has served during its long voyage of 300 years. Various Battle Honours are engraved on the central pillar.

In this manner the Patialas continue to strive to attain best results in various fields. Its rise during the past 300 years has been phenomenal, and there's no looking back for the Patialas who are focused on a challenging future, in constant pursuit of excellence, true to their motto-'Khalsa Ji Ki Fateh!'

15
Other Fronts

Apart from operational achievements, 15 Punjab (Patiala) has also carved out a niche for itself in various other fronts, be it operational exercises, sports, adventure / humanitarian activities, organizing rallies and so on. While a substantial amount has already been written about such achievements in the preceding chapters, a few are being highlighted in this chapter.

Coming to rallies, 15 Punjab (Patiala) organised the Punjab Regiment Ex-Servicemen's Rally on 2 November 1991 at Jammu. More than expected number of ex-Galleymen attended the function, which was also attended by dignitaries like Lieutenant General DSR Sahni, GOC-in-C Northern Command, Lieutenant General VR Raghavan, the then Chief of Staff 16 Corps and Colonel of the Punjab Regiment, and Lieutenant General Shankar Roy Choudhary, the then GOC 16 Corps. The rally was addressed by Lieutenant General DSR Sahni, who has gone a record to state that it was amongst the best rallies that he had attended. During 2002 the unit organised another successful rally at Sri Ganganagar, which was the talk of town for a long time.

In the sphere of turnout and drill, the tall and smart soldiers of 1st Patiala always stood out wherever they went, and many senior formation commanders often made a bid for the battalion ceremonial guards at their respective flag staff houses, or for ceremonial occasions. Till Kanpur the unit's ceremonial dress comprised a maroon turban. A metal band or 'Chakkar' was affixed around the turban, albeit at a slant, in a pattern akin to the ceremonial headgear worn by the Sikh or Sikh Light Infantry troops. The turnout was very impressive, to say the least, and it is hoped that the tradition continues in right earnest.

It is also a matter of pride that, for the regimental contingent which stood first in the Republic Day parade of 1993, twelve of the 14 soldiers sent by 15 Punjab (Patiala) formed part of the marching contingent, which speaks volumes of the Patiala drill and turnout.

While at Kanpur, 15 Punjab (Patiala), which had moved from Baramulla where it had established a splendid record in counter insurgency operations, performed exceedingly well once again. It remained a forerunner in the prestigious 1 Corps exercises named 'Paschim Vijay', 'Grand Slam' and 'Vijay Prahar' during its tenure there from early 1995 to mid 1998. The battalion also had the rare distinction of not only lifting a vast majority of the inter battalion and formation sports and professional competitions, but were also proud winners of the 4 Infantry Divisional Anti Tank, Mortar and Ghatak competitions on a number of occasions. The unit had also adopted a 'Mahila Ashram' for destitute and orphaned girls and an 'Anath Ashram' for orphaned boys, for which the unit provided all the inmates with cooked food, clothing, toiletries and other basic requirements and amenities regularly. This noble charitable work had been highly appreciated and commended by one and all, both within and out of uniform. That apart, a weapon and equipment display was also organised for the children of various Kanpur schools which was an instant hit with the students, both boys and girls.

Coming to safaris and expeditions, 15 Punjab (Patiala) were not to be left behind. While at Kanpur, its team under Major Siddharth Ranjan took part in the Red Eagle Jonga Safari covering a distance of 7500 kms from 10 October '97 to 1 November 1997. This battalion's team also took part in the 62 Infantry Brigade cycle expedition from 15 to 23 December 1997 under Major Amit Sehgal, covering a total distance of 477 km from Kanpur to Khajuraho and back. To coincide with its tercentenary, the unit is all set to launch a motorcycle expedition from Gobindgarh to the famous town of Kaja in Himachal Pradesh. The expedition will negotiate some difficult mountainous stretches en route.

During its field tenure in Sunderbani under the command of Colonel R.R. Nimbhorkar, SM, the unit celebrated its golden jubilee of the battle of Zojila on 31 October - 1 November 1998. Inspite of heavy operational commitments of the battalion in this sector, the function was a resounding success. Amongst those who attended were Major General S.K. Awasthy, the then Colonel of the Punjab Regiment; Major General Lakshman Singh Lehal (retired), who has had a close association with the battalion throughout; Brigadier Sukhdev Singh, VrC, MC (retired), the commanding officer and hero of the battle of Zojila; Major General Tej Pathak, GOC 10 Infantry division and numerous other dignitaries and officers, both serving and retired.

Such activities of the battalion only stand to highlight the tremendous versatility of the Patialas in varied fields, and there is no doubt that the battalion will keep excelling in a greater variety of spheres in the years to come, as a result of its well established and time tested norms and traditions.

They fought to win wars
With infinite fury,
Through grit and guts they assured,
A deckful of glory!

TRAINING FOR A STRIKE ROLE

With and against armour

(Photos by Col Anil Shorey)

Preparing for canal crossing

(Photos by Col Anil Shorey)

A foot and mobile column operating in the desert sector

An innovative training aid being tested successfully

(Photos by Col Anil Shorey)

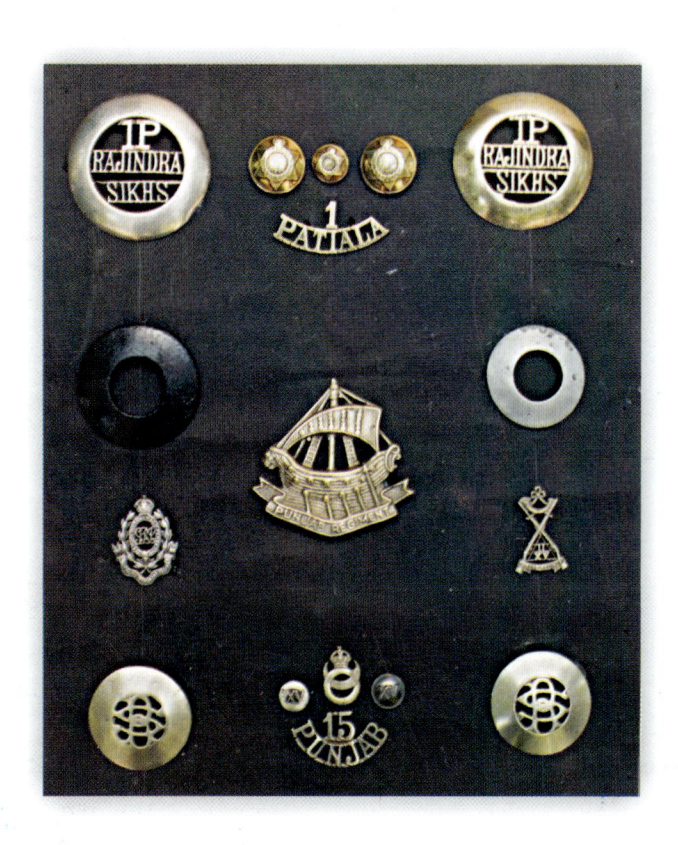

A rare collection of 1st Patiala and 15 Punjab badges

(Photo & collection Col Anil Shorey)

A MATTER OF HONOUR

Naik Bhuri Singh proudly stands next to the prized War Trophy at unit Quarter Guard at Kanpur. He was one of the soldiers who captured this Pakistani 3.7 Howitzer at Zojila

The unit's legendary concentration during the 1Corps exercise- "Operation Paschim Vijay"- 1996

(Photos by Col Anil Shorey)

Brigadier Sukhdev Singh, MC, VrC (retd.), unveils the sterling silver Zojila Trophy at Kanpur on Zojila Day - 1996. Also seen in picture are Lt Gen GS Brar, AVSM, Colonel of the Regiment alongwith the then CO, Col Anil Shorey

An artists conception of the Tercentenary Trophy—1705 - 2005

The proud winners of the coveted 4 Infantry Divisional 'Ghatak' Championship Trophy - 1997

School children of Kanpur on a motivation cum familiarization visit to 15 Punjab (Patiala) -1997

(Photos by Col Anil Shorey)

THE MAHARAJAS

BABA ALA SINGH
(1705-1765)

AMAR SINGH
(1765-1781)

SAHIB SINGH
(1781-1813)

KARAM SINGH
(1813-1845)

NARINDER SINGH
(1845-1862)

MOHINDER SINGH
(1862-1876)

RAJINDER SINGH
(1876-1900)

BHUPINDER SINGH
(1900-1938)

YADVINDER SINGH
(1938 - POST INDEPENDENCE)

AMARINDER SINGH

Epilogue

If one was to condense the achievements of 15 Punjab (Patiala) in a more comprehensive form, one would fail to find the right words to explain its splendid performance. One would also run out of suitable adjectives to describe this legendary battalion and its legendary troops, as was the case with me. Suffice to say that the unit has always and will continue to function as a 'live wire' battalion.

Take the case of honours and awards. It has established a record which is second best in the Indian army. Except for 1 Sikh battalion, which is now designated as 4 Mech (Sikh), no other battalion of the Indian army is able to come anywhere near the record established by 15 Punjab (Patiala). This Epilogue intends to highlight various aspects of the battalion, through prose and verse, related to its merit, customs and traditions, apart from listing out the proud commanding officers who have ensured that the battalion continues to maintain even higher goals with every command tenure.

"They forge on ahead like never before,
With renewed zest and vigour.
1st Patiala shall remain the best,
As a symbol of Truth and Valour".

Epilogue

Gallantry Award Winners
World War Two

Lieutenant General Balwant Singh Sidhu	-	CBE, DSO
Brigadier Bikramdev Singh Gill	-	DSO
Brigadier Dalip Singh	-	MBE
Brigadier Sukhdev Singh	-	MC
Major Kuldip Singh	-	MC
Major Baldev Singh	-	MC
Subedar Major Rakha Singh	-	MC
Subedar Ajmer Singh	-	MC
Subedar Darbara Singh	-	MC
Subedar Charan Singh	-	MC
Naib Subedar Amir Singh	-	MC
Naib Subedar Sarwan Singh	-	MC
Lance Naik Bahadur Singh	-	IOM
CHM Gurbax Singh	-	MM
CHM Mohinder Singh	-	MM
Havildar (later Subedar) Malkiat Singh	-	MM
Havildar Gurnam Singh	-	MM
Naik Sucha Singh	-	MM
Naik Bir Singh	-	MM
Naik Joginder Singh	-	MM
Sepoy Jang Singh	-	MM
Sepoy Telu Singh	-	MM
Sepoy Karnail Singh	-	MM
Naib Subedar Mangal Singh	-	IDSM
Naib Subedar Jagir Singh	-	IDSM
Havildar Dalip Singh	-	IDSM

Naik Atma Singh	-	IDSM
Sepoy Kaka Singh	-	IDSM
Sepoy Cook Jagat Singh	-	BEM
OBI CL – I	-	2
OBI CL – II	-	3
Mention-in-Despatches	-	54
Commendation Card by C-in-C	-	5
Commendation Card by District Commander	-	1

Jammu and Kashmir Operations – 1947-48

Subedar Gurdial Singh	MVC
Subedar Sapuran Singh	MVC
Naib Subedar Hardev Singh	MVC
Naib Subedar Lal Singh	MVC
Naik Pritam Singh	MVC
Naik Amar Singh	MVC
Naik Hari Singh	MVC
Porter Mohd Ismail	MVC
Brigadier Sukhdev Singh	VrC
Major Joginder Singh	VrC
Subedar Sant Singh	VrC
Naib Subedar Balwant Singh	VrC
BHM Sewa Singh	VrC
Lance Naik Phuman Singh	VrC
CHM Mukand Singh	VrC
BHM Chet Singh	VrC
Havildar Gurdial Singh	VrC

Epilogue

Naik Mehar Singh	VrC
Naik Sajjan Singh	VrC
Lance Naik Naurang Singh	VrC
Naik Chand Singh	VrC
Sepoy Gajjan Singh	VrC
Sepoy Teja Singh (Posthumous)	VrC
Sepoy Hazara Singh (Posthumous)	VrC
Sepoy Zaila Singh (Posthumous)	VrC
Sepoy Bachan Singh (Posthumous)	VrC
Mentioned-in-Despatches	-34
Commendation Cards by C-in-C	-42

Breakdown of Total Decorations

World War 1

Indian Order of Merit	4
Order of British India Second Class	5
Indian Distinguished Service Medal	8
Mentioned-in-Despatches	21
Indian Meritorious Service Medal	10
Order of King George (with sword) First Class	1
Order of King George (with sword) Fourth Class	1
Serbian Gold Medal	1

Serbian Silver Medal	1
Order of the Nile Fourth Class	1
	53

World War II

CBE	1
DSO	2
MBE	1
MC	9
IOM	1
MM	10
IDSM	5
OBE CL – I	2
OBE CL – II	3
Mentioned-in-Despatches	54
Commendation Cards C-in-C	5
BEM	1
Commendation Cards District Commander	1
	95

Zojila Ops – 1948

Maha Vir Chakra	8
Vir Chakra	18
Mentioned-in-Despatches	34
Commendation Cards	42
	102

Epilogue

1949 – 1987

Shaurya Chakra	1
COAS's Commendation Cards	8
	9

Intrusion Dalunang

Yudh Seva Medal	1
Sena Medal	4
Mentioned-in-Despatches	1
COAS's Commendation Cards	3
GOC-in-C's Commendation Cards	5
	14

CI Ops : Op Rakshak

Kirit Chakra	1
Shaurya Chakra	2
Sena Medal	12
COAS's Commendation Cards	17
GOC-in-C's Commendation Cards	29
COAS's Unit Citation	1
GOC-in-C's Unit Appreciation	1
	63

Kanpur

GOC-in-C's Commendation Card	1
Grand Total	**337**

Battle Honours of 15 Punjab (Patiala)

Battle	Year
Barnala	1723
Bhatti War	1738
Sirhind	1761
Maler Kotla	1767
Pinjore	1768
Bhatinda	1771
Marhatta War	1784
Gorkha War	1814
Sikh War	1845
Lajwana	1854
Independence War	1857
Afghanistan	1878
Tiraha	1897
Suez Canal	1915
Gaza	1917
Gallipoli	1918
Afghanistan	1919
Waziristan	1940
Burma	1942
Malaya	1945
Java	1945
Zojila	1948

Theatre/Other Honours

Punjab '71	1971
COAS Unit Citation (Baramula)	1993

Epilogue

The Commanding Officers

Kumaidan Gazi Beg	1783-1822
Kumaidan Dharam Singh	1823-1842
Kumaidan Gajjan Singh	1843-1855
Colonel Amir Khan	1856-1889
Colonel Bahadur Ali	1890-1896
Colonel SB Sunder Singh, OBI	1897-1912
Colonel Gurbakhsh Singh Jeji	1913-1917
Colonel Ishar Singh Bahadur, OBI	1918-1921
Colonel SB Gurdial Singh Harika, OBI, DSO, CIE	1922-1933
Colonel Balwant Singh Sidhu Bahadur, CBE, DSO, OBI	1934-1944
Lieutenant Colonel Bikramdev Singh Gill, DSO	1944-1948
Lieutenant Colonel Sukhdev Singh, MC, VrC	1948-1951
Lieutenant Colonel Gurcharan Singh, MC	1952-1955
Lieutenant Colonel VS Jog	1955-1960
Lieutenant Colonel JS Mandaher	1960-1963
Lieutenant Colonel HS Kullar	1963-1966
Lieutenant Colonel CS Dosanj	1966-1968

Lieutenant Colonel JS Sandhu	1968-1970
Lieutenant Colonel GBVL Sastry	1970-1972
Lieutenant Colonel VR Raghavan	1972-1975
Lieutenant Colonel Rajinder Singh	1975-1979
Lieutenant Colonel BS Grewal	1979-1981
Lieutenant Colonel Shivdev Singh	1981-1983
Colonel HS Brar	1983-1986
Colonel S Hoon	1986-1987
Colonel MS Sibia, YSM	1987-1990
Colonel MS Kalra	1990-1993
Colonel KS Aithmian, SM	1993-1995
Colonel Anil Shorey	1995-1998
Colonel RR Nimbhorkar, SM	1998-2001
Colonel Dipender Sarin	2001-2004
Colonel Advitya Madan	2004-till date

Epilogue

'Savaiya (Prayer)'

Deh Siva Bar Mohe Ehey
Subh Karman Te Kabhun Na Taron,
Na Daron Ar So Jab Jaiye Laron
Nischay Kar Apni Jeet Karon.
Ar Sikh Hon Apne Hi Man Kau
Eh Lalach Gou Gun Tau Uchron
Jab Aav Ki Audh Nidhan Banay
Att Hi Ran Mein Tab Jujh Maron.

The above is a 1st Patiala prayer (Savaiya) which the unit recites everyday before undertaking the daily chores/ any special task/operation. Its English translation reads:

"Grant Me, O Lord
This Boon
That I May Not Falter
In Doing Good,
Nor Do I Have Fear
In My Heart
When Fighting In The Battlefield.
May I Always Have
Pure Thoughts In My Mind
And Never Be Tempted Be Greed
And When My End Shall Come
May I Die Fighting In The Battlefield."

Ballad of First Patiala
(A Unit History in Verse)

In 1705 a force was formed,
Baba Ala Singh was founder.
Dera Formation's coat it adorned,
As Patiala State's defender.

It fought wars in distant places,
Like Barnala, Bhatinda and Sirhind.
Its fame spread at rapid paces
Across Gwalior, Pinjore and Jind.

On a French Model the unit took
Under Kumaidan Gazi Beg.
Maharaja Rajinder Singh changed its look
And refined its vintage gait.
In Wolrd War One it fought abroad,
In Suez and Gallipoli.
It fought with the elite Maghdoba Force,
At Gaza and Mitla Valley.

It showed its grit in World War Two,
In Burma and Waziristan.
Malaya and Batavia were theatres new,
Where the unit showed great élan.

No sooner they returned to Patiala,
They dealth with partition pangs.
Following Pak's attack on India,
In Kashmir they took a stand.

At Chhamb and Jhanghar they showed thier mettle,
At Naoshera they showed their clout.

Epilogue

But indeed their finest battle,
At Zojila did make us proud.

Under Sukhdev Singh's able grip,
They fought the Gilgit Scouts.
Enemy's defences they soon ripped,
And Pakis were on the rout.

MVCs Eight and VrCs 18
They won in J&K.
Tough and lean, a winning team,
Were the Patialas all the way.

In 1950 it joined the fold,
Of the oldest Punjab Regiment.
It remained atop, always bold,
As 15 Punjab the magnificent.
In 71 war at Hussainiwala,
When a Pak Brigade had assaulted,
Through determination and sheer valour,
Three of its attacks they halted.

It again excelled in Dalunang,
Dras and China Border.
Baramulla's militant and foreign gangs,
Were crushed to restore order.

Honours and Awards its won are many,
A total of Three Twenty Four.
A Unit Citation in the Valley,
Has further increased its score.

'Khalsa ji ki Fateh' – a motto proud,
'Khanda' and sword are charms.

'Wahe Guru ki Fateh' is cried aloud,
Shining is their Coat of Arms.

Senior officers its produced are many,
Gurdial, Balwant and Kullar.
Raghavan and Shivdev, all uncanny,
Our pride – these Patiala pillars!!

They forge on ahead like never before,
With renewed zest and vigour.
1st Patiala shall remain the best,
As a symbol of Truth and Valour.

'Wahe Guru ji ka Khalsa
Wahe Guru ji ki Fateh'.

—by Col Anil Shorey

Index

Afghan front 71
Afridi tribesmen 39
Aithmian, Colonel K.S. 182
Akhand Path 83
Akhnoor 109, 180
Allenby, Field Marshal Lord 50, 51
Ambala Brigade 72
Amman 51
Andaman and Nicobar group of islands 82
Arawa 81
Archduke Francis Ferdinand of Austria 42
Asia Minor 73
Awami League 156
Awasthy, Major General S.K. 207
Axis Powers 43

Bahadur, Colonel Gurbux Singh Jeji 43
Bahadur, Colonel Ishwar Singh 46
Baisakhi day 33
Bakshi, Captain N. 184
Banihal Pass 97
Baramula, taming of 182
Barnala 30
battalion, re-modelling of the 33
Batavia 83
Bathinda 32

Battle of Plassey 18
Beg, Gazi 33
Beg, Ghani 33
Bhardwaj, Captain V. 184
Bhagat (now known as Solan) 36
Bhatti Chiefs 32
Bhatti Wars 31
Border Security Force 162, 179
Brachil Pass in the Kargil sector 26
Brigade 74
British 'Red Coats' 18
British 81
British East India Company 17
British Expeditionary Force (BEF) 42
British Indian Army 87
British model, Indian Army based on the 21
Burma Army 75
Burma, dense rain jungles of 87
Borneo 83

Calcultta, Patialas moved to 154
Campbell, Captain H. 43
Cariappa, Lieutenant General K.M. 142
Carnatic Battalion 19
Ceylon 82
Chail 36
Chak Amru 26

Index

Operation Bison 122
Operation Duck 120
Operation Gulmarg 96, 97, 99
'Operation Pawan' in Sri Lanka 26
Order of King George 53
Order of the British Empire 50
Order of the Nile Fourth Class 53

Pakistan 23, 96, 103, 160
   game plan 184
   psyche of the military leaders of 177
Pakistani attacks at Kalidhar 25
Pakistani Chaffee tanks 26
Pakistani raiders 109
Palestine front 45
Parachute Regiment 24
Pathak, Major General Tej 207
Pathans 106
   the wily 87
Patialas 80, 104, 108, 109, 110, 114, 121, 124, 154, 166, 173, 182, 203, 30, 87
   in World War II 73
   tremendous versatility of the 207
Pearl Harbour 73
PEPSU 25
Peshawar 97
Phul Dynasty 27
Phul, Chowdhury 27
Phulkian House 46
Phulkian States 27
Pir Panjal Range 179
Pirthil Nakka 113
POK 181
Pondicherry, French town of 18
Poonch sector 26
Port Dickson, Patialas arrived at 83

Port Said 43
Prince of the Wales 71
Princely Indian States 21
Proxy War 177
Punjab Regiment 19
Punjab Regiment (Patiala) 26, 152
Punjab Regiment Ex-Servicemen's Rally 205
Punjab Regiment of India and Pakistan 24
Punjab Regiment, history of the 17
Punjab, combatting terrorism in 26
Punjabis 20
Purukh, Akal 46

Qajser Hind 164

Raghavan, Lieutenant Colonel V.R. 169, 205
Rahman, Sheikh Mujibur 156
Rajouri 98
Rajputs 20
Ranjan, Major Siddharth 207
Rashtriya Rifles (RR) 25
Rawalpindi 97
Razmak 74
Red Eagle Jonga Safar 207
Robert Clive 18
Routh, Captain G.S.F 43

Sahib Kaur, Bibi 34
Sahni, Lieutenant General D.S.R. 205
Saini, Captain A.175
Samadhi Tower 164
Sandhu, Lieutenant Colonel J.S. 155
Sarin, Lieutenant Colonel Dipendra 85
Scindias of Gwalior 34
Scott, Major General H.L. 98

Kaur, Maharani Hukum 33
Khalsa 47
Khan, Kumaidan Amir 37
Khan, Brigadier Mohammad Aziz 173
Khan, General Yahya 157
Khan, Zain, the Governor of Sirhind 31
Khem Karan 169
Khulna 26
Khurram Force 70
Kitchener, Lord 20
Knight Grand Cross 50
Kohima, Japanese bid on 79
Kohima-Imphal road, Japanese cut 78
Kumaidan, title of 33

Ladakh 98
Lal Paltan 18
Lal, Captain Mohinder 202
Lawrence, Major Stringer 18
Lehal, Major General Lakshman Singh 207
Line of Control 182, 184
Longowal 26, 29

Machhoi in Jammu & Kashmir 131
Madras Native Infantry 20
Madras Presidency 19
Maghdeba Column 45
Maha Vir Chakra (MVC) 110
Maharaja of Bikaner 49
Maharaja of Patiala 71
Maharaja Scindia 38
Malaya 84
Manawar Ki Tawi, a fast flowing river 103
Mandher, Lietenant Colonel J.S. 153
Marathas 20, 33

Mehta, Lieutenant General S.S. 203
Mesopotamia 52
   1 Patiala Lancers moved to 44
Military Cross (MC) 53
Minimarg 173
Mitla Pass Mobile Column 45
Mobile Patiala 109
Moplahs 20
Motibagh Palace 71
Mountbatten, Lord Louis 81
Mughal Empire 28
Muslim majority battalions 23

Nagasaki, dropping of atom bombs by the US Air Force at 81
Naha Akal Infantry 23
Nalagarh 35
Nand Mal 34
Nasta Chun Pass 153
Nazi Germany 73
NEFA 25
Nehru, Jawaharlal 121
Nimbhorkar, Colonel 185
   9 Jat 21
   19 Hyderabad 21
North West Frontier Province (NWFP) 22, 43, 74
Noushera 109

1 (Strike Corps) 183
1/5 Gurkha Rifles 120, 121
1/14 Punjab Regiment 24
Op Ablaze 154
Op Blue Star 170
Op Cactus Lilly 157
Op Meghdoot 180
Op Parakram 202
Op Rakshak 182
Op Riddle 154
Op Vijay 180

Index

Garhwal 20
Garibpur battle 26
Gaza 25, 51
General Lord Rawlington's Grand Reorganisation 21
George Cross 85
Ghatak platoon 184
Gilgit Scouts 119
Gill, Colonel Bikramdev Siingh 83
Gorkha War 35
Grand Cross of the Order of Nile 51
Gumri in Jammu & Kashmir 130
Guru Gobind Singh 28

Hansi 32
Hari Singh, Maharaja 96
Hasan, Khalifa Mohammad 38
Hindu and Sikh refugees 100
Hiroshima, dropping of atom bombs by the US Air Force at 81
Hissar 32
Hitler 73
Hoon, Colonel S. 171
Howitzers 120
Hukum Kaur, Maharani, 33
Hussain, Dr. Zakir 17 President 155
Hussainiwala, battle of 159,169
Hyderabad Police action 25

Imperial Government 40
Imperial Service Troops 22
Imperial War Cabinet 49
Imperial War Conference 49, 50
Indian Army, Evolution of 17
Indian Army, father of the 18
Indian calender, Baisakhi day by the 33

Indian Distinguished Service Medal (IDSM) 53
Indian Meritorious Service Medal (IMSM) 53
Indian Mutiny 37
Indian Order ot Merit (IOM) 53
Indian State Forces War Establishment Interim Scheme of 1920, 71
Indo-Burma frontier 74
Indonesia 83
Indo-Pak War 1971, 155, 156
Instrument of Accession, Maharaja Sri Hari Singh signed the 100
Ismail, Mohammad 127

Jaisal, Rajput Chief 27
Jammu & Kashmir (J&K) 96, 105, 153
  combatting terrorism in 26
  15 Punjab (then known as 1st Patiala saved) 25
Jamuna 32
Jat tribes 29
Java, 83
Jessore 26
Jhangar, recapture of 112
Jordan Valley 45

Kabar Masjid Kajahir 47
Kabaw Valley 77
Kaithal Rebellion of 1843, 36
Kaksar 175
Karachi 51
Kargil 98, 119
Kargil War 184
Kashmir Operation 25
Kashmir problem 177
Katoch, Brigadier J.C 101
Kaur, Bibi Sahib 34

Chatha, Lieutenant Colonel Ahmed 172
Chaytor's Force, First Patiala formed part of 47
Chhamb 107
Chhamb, Battle of 103
Chhogil Canal, battle for the 25
China, 1962 war against 25
Chindwin River 75
Chinese aggression 154
Coote, Sir Eyre 20
Choudhary, Major D. 184, 185
Choudhary, Lieutenant General Shankar Roy 205
Cis-Sutlej area 35
Cis-Sutlej Sikhs 31
Ochterlonly, Colonel 35
Commander British Empire (CBE) 87
Commanding Officers, 223

Dacca 157
Dalunang, Battle of 172
Dera Formation 31
Doda 98, 180
Dogar, Bakshi Lakhna 28
Dogras 20
Dosanj, Lieutenant Colonel C.S. 154
Dras, capture of 124
Durrani, Ahmed Shah 31
Dutch East Indies 83

East India Company 18, 19, 30
East Pakistan 156
East Punjab State's Union (PEPSU) 23
8 Punjab 21
8/12 FF Regiment 24
1812 Light Regiment 185
80 Independent Brigade Group 108

18 Garhwal 21
11 Sikh 21
El-Houd 47

Fatehabad 32
Fernandes, George 203
15 Battalion the Punjab Regiment (Patiala) 27
15 Ludhiana Sikhs 50
15 Punjab (Patiala) 17, 21, 23, 158, 182, 185, 205
    300 year old battalion 26
50 Parachute Brigade 102, 112
1st (Abbottabad) Indian Infantry Brigade 86
1st Mahar (MG) 101
1st Patiala Infantry 73
1st Patiala Lancers 44
1st Patiala Rajindra Sikh Infantry 71, 74, 122
1st Patiala, Inception of 27
1st Patiala Imperial Service Infantry (Rajindra Sikh) 40
1st Punjab Regiment 20
1st Sikh War of 1845-47, 36
1st Wingate Expedition 77
5/12 Frontier Force Regiment (FF) 24
5 Maratha Light Infantry 21, 120
Forsyth, Sir Douglas 38
14 Punjab (Nabha Akal) 21, 23, 26
4 Jammu and Kashmir Rifles 99
4 Grenediers 21
4 Kumaon 101
4 Rajput 121
French army 33
    infantry battalion model 33

G.C.S.I. (Grand Cross for Services in India) 40
Gallantry Award Winners 217

2nd Punjab Regiment 19
   Consisted of Sikh, Dogras,
     Punjabi Mussalmans 23
2nd Sikh War 37
Sehgal, Major Amit 207
Sen, Brigadier L.P. 101
Serbs 42
Serbian Gold Medal 53
   Silver Medal 53
7 Rajput 21
17 Dogra 21
79 Mountain Brigade 182
77 Brigade 121
72 Hired Camel Corps 44
Shakargarh area 26
Shamsher, Major 107
Sharma, Major Somnath 101
Sharma, Lieutenant Vikas 202
Shia Muslim 180
Shiwalik Hills 72
Sholinghur, first Battle Honour 20
Shorey, Colonel Anil 26, 183
Shoulder, the Patiala post 126
Siachen Glacier 180
Sidhu clan 27
Sidhu, Colonel Balwant Singh 74
Sikh Confederacy 27
Sikh-Dogra composition 24
Sikh-Dogra pattern 24
Sikhs 20 Jats 20
Simla 36
Simla Accord 168
Singh, Lance Naik Chand 134
Singh, Subedar Kahla 52
Singh, Lieutenant Colonel
   Rajinder 169
Singh, Sepoy Amar 130
Singh, Baba Ala, the rightful
   founder of Patiala State 30
Singh, Sepoy Bachan 137

Singh, Bakshish, 19 years old
   sepoy named 85
Singh, Naib Subedar Balwant 132
Singh, Bhagat 160
Singh, Maharaja Bhupinder 70
Singh, Lance Naik Chand 138
Singh, Chet, Naik 12, 22
Singh, Dharam 33
Singh, Sepoy Gajjan 33, 134
Singh, Lieutenant Colonel
   Gurcharan 152
Singh, Colonel Harbaksh 101
Singh, Jemadar Hardev 129
Singh, Sepoy Hardial 126
Singh, Sepoy Hari 116
Singh, Captain Hazura 107
Singh, Subedar Jagir 184
Singh, Jodha 32
Singh, Major Joginder 116
Singh, Major General Kalwant 101
Singh, Lieutenant General
   Kulwant 108
Singh, Maharaja Bhupinder 40, 41
Singh, Naik Mehar 116, 117
Singh, Havildar Mukand 133, 139
Singh, Lance Naik Naurang 116
Singh, Lance Naik Phuman 106
Singh, Naik Pritam 130
Singh, Raja Ala 29
Singh, Raja Karam 35
Singh, Brigadier Rajinder 100
Singh, Lance Naik Sajjan 133
Singh, Jemadar Sampooran 128
Singh, Subedar Sant 131
Singh, Brigadier Sukhdev 207
Singh, Lieutenant Colonel
   Sukhdev 122, 142
Singh, Captain Tejvir 184
Singh, Sepoy Zaila 136
Sirsa 32

Index

6/13 FF Rifles 24
6 Rajputana Rifles 21
16 Punjab (Patiala) 21, 23
69 Mountain Brigade 169
62 Infantry Brigade cycle expedition 207
62 Infantry Brigade of 183
Skardu 119
Slim, Field Marshal 80
South East Asia Command (SEAC) 81
Sri Ganganagar 205
Srinagar, Zojila Pass linking 119
Stalin's forces in Russia 73
Standstill Agreement 96
State Armies like those of Travancore, Cochin, Mysore, Kolhapur, Hyderabad, Berar, Indore, Baroda, Gwalior, Bhopal, Saurashtra, Jaipur, Jodhpur, Faridkot, Patiala, Jind, Nabha, Kapurthala, Cooch Behar, Kashmir 22
Subsidiary Alliance 22
Suez Canal 43
Sumatra 83
Sunni Muslim 180
Sutlej 32
Swat valley 40

Ten Baluch 21
Tenga Valley 170
Thakkar, B.S. 203
Thapa, General Amar Singh 35
13 Frontier Force Rifles 21
3 Afghan War 70
13 Punjab (Jind) 23
32 Imperial Service Brigade 43
32 Mountain Brigade 154
3 Grenadiers 185

3 Jat 120
3 Madras 21
3 Maratha Light Infantry 113
3 Northern Light Infantry (NLI)
Tochi Valley operations 74
Turkish Army, operations against the 43
12 Frontier Force Regiment 21
29 Infantry Brigade 169
Twin Pimples, enemy post 126
2 Maratha Light Infantry 183
2/3 Gorkha Rifles 109

Udhampur 180
United Nations Emergency Force (UNEF) 26
United Nations Peace Keeping Operations 25
Usman, Brigadier 112

Vir Chakra (VrC) 110, 106

Wagah Border 159
Waraich, Major S.P.S. 161
Waziristan 74
West Pakistan 156
Wellesley, Lord 22
World War I, 42, 52
World War II, 141

Yog, V.S., Colonel 153
Yol Camp (Kangra Valley) 152
Yudh Seva Medal (YSM) 176

Zakir Hussain, Dr. 17
President 155
Zojila Pass 119, 121, 132
Zojila, epic battle of 171
Zojila, Frozen Heights of, 25, 118